SECRET
SCARS

SECRET SCARS

*Uncovering and Understanding
the Addiction of Self-Injury*

V. J. Turner

Hazelden
Center City, Minnesota 55012-0176

1-800-328-0094
1-651-213-4590 (Fax)
www.hazelden.org

Library of Congress Cataloging-in-Publication Data
Turner, V. J., 1961–
   Secret scars : uncovering and understanding the addiction of
     self-injury / V. J. Turner.
     p. cm.
   Includes bibliographical references and index.
   ISBN 1-56838-914-0 (softcover)
     1. Self-injurous behavior. 2. Teenage girls—Mental health.
     3. Self-mutilation. I. Title.
  RJ506.S44 T874 2002
  616.85'82—dc21

                                            2002068636

06 05 04 03 02   6 5 4 3 2 1

Editor's note
All of the stories in this book are based on actual experiences. The
names and details have been changed to protect the privacy of the
people involved. In some cases, composites have been created.

The Twelve Steps are reprinted and adapted with permission of
Alcoholics Anonymous World Services, Inc. (AAWS). Permission to
reprint and adapt the Twelve Steps does not mean that AAWS has reviewed or approved the contents of this publication, or that AAWS
necessarily agrees with the views expressed herein. AA is a program
of recovery from alcoholism *only*—use of the Twelve Steps in connection with programs and activities which are patterned after AA, but
which address other problems, or in any other non-AA context, does
not imply otherwise.

Cover design by Theresa Gedig
Interior design by Rachel Holscher
Typesetting by Stanton Publication Services, Inc.

*This book is dedicated to self-injurers and all other addicts,
especially to those who are still struggling.*

Contents

Introduction

There is hope; there are solutions . . .

The purpose of this book is to offer hope and solutions to the problem of self-injury. It is for those who self-injure and for the people in their lives who care.

In this book we will define self-injury as intentionally physically harming yourself to cope with painful emotions. Self-injury is often misunderstood and information is scarce. Few people know what self-injury is or can explain it in commonsense terms.

Some medical and mental health professionals and experts believe that self-injury is the fastest growing problem among teenagers. Many different terms are used to describe this disorder, including self-mutilation; the self-injurious behavior syndrome (SIBS); and the deliberate self-harm syndrome. The term "cutter" is often used to describe self-injurers because cutting is the most common method used. In this book, we will refer to this disorder as the self-injurious behavior syndrome. We will refer to people who have this disorder as self-injurers.

A study in the late 1990s, in which more than eight hundred high school psychologists in the state of California were interviewed, revealed that each psychologist knew of at least two or three students per school who self-injured. Those were only the ones that they were aware of. A *New York Times Magazine* article, entitled "Power Suffering"

1

(Egan 1999), stated that in America, "about two million people, mostly women, cut and burn themselves compulsively in pursuit of an illusory sense of control."

Self-injury is a hidden disorder, much like bulimia, which may go entirely unnoticed for years. It is usually kept well hidden from others, including medical and mental health professionals. Self-injurers are usually in denial that they have a problem. Consequently, statistics grossly underestimate the actual occurrence of self-injury.

In addition to teenagers, there are also many adults who suffer in silence from this affliction, usually over the course of many years, beginning in childhood or adolescence. Self-injury is far more prevalent in females than in males. Therefore, throughout the book, when referring to self-injurers the gender pronouns "she" and "her" are used. This is not to imply that males do not self-injure. Male self-injurers are most often found in confined settings such as juvenile halls, correctional facilities, and youth residential treatment centers. Case studies of male self-injurers are included in this book as well.

When it comes to what to do to help a teenager who repeatedly cuts or burns herself on purpose and just can't stop, her parents, schoolteachers, counselors, friends, and she herself are at a loss . . .

What is known—and especially what can help—is here for you in this book. What is unique about my approach is that the self-injurious behavior syndrome is addressed as an *addiction*. This has been alluded to numerous times in the clinical and research literature, as well as in information presented to the general public. However, no one has—until now—fully developed and explained the theoretical point of view from an addictions standpoint, or applied it to practical approaches to treatment. That is what this groundbreaking book does.

Secret Scars: Uncovering and Understanding the Addiction of Self-Injury clearly explains how the problem of self-injury can be treated in many of the same ways that are known to work for other addictions, such as for alcohol and drugs. This book is clinically sound, well-grounded in the research literature, user-friendly, interesting, practical, *and* deeply inspirational. The primary focus is on getting out of the problem and into the solution.

In addition to my academic and clinical credentials and many years of experience in working therapeutically with teenagers and patients with addictive disorders, I also have my own personal experience with and successful recovery from the self-injurious behavior syndrome.

I have suffered from this affliction since childhood, starting at about six years old. It continued to get progressively worse, especially during my teenage years. There is one incident I recall—I know it was in the first grade because I remember the nun who was my teacher at the time—in which my parents were arguing at the dinner table. It was beginning to get loud and violent, and I was afraid that my father would hurt my mother. I was in a daze and didn't realize what I was doing until my mother looked over at me, horrified, and asked me why I scratched my face with my fingernails. I remember running upstairs, climbing onto the bathroom counter to look in the mirror, and seeing the scratch marks and the bleeding, and thinking to myself, "At least it stopped them from fighting."

I also remember going through my mother's old wooden sewing box and finding safety pins, needles, and other things to hurt myself with. They made some interesting sewing implements in the 1960s that worked quite well. By the time I was eleven or twelve, I was cutting my arms with razor blades and burning my hand with a light bulb from a turned-over bedside lamp, the lamp with the angels on it, so at least I could think peaceful thoughts before I fell asleep.

Like many others who suffer from the problem of self-injury, I, too, had an extraordinarily difficult childhood and adolescence, enduring the death of my mother from cancer when I was ten years old, growing up in a family environment of alcoholism and domestic violence, and having been subjected to severe physical and emotional abuse over the course of many years as a child. Like many other self-injurers, I also had an eating disorder, anorexia nervosa, as a teenager in the early 1970s. I recovered by participating in an in-patient hospital program that was heavily based on behavior modification. Consequences and removal of privileges for not eating were emphasized. I was also given medical care, including nutritional counseling, and individual and peer group therapy with other teenagers on the unit who had a variety of medical, psychiatric, and severe drug addiction problems. I have recovered successfully from anorexia with no episodes of relapse over the last twenty-five years.

While successfully recovering from anorexia, my problem with self-injury did not go away. It carried on well into my college years and into adulthood, although no one knew about it—not even college roommates living in the same dorm—other than those whom I told directly. It was a faulty and destructive coping mechanism for whenever life got tough, or to get through another final exam, or for times when the emotional pain of the past became too overwhelming. And eventually, I became increasingly addicted to the "high," which became more important to me than anything else. On the outside, I was viewed as a high achiever, very successful in academics and in my career. On the inside, I suffered in silence. Especially during the last few years of my active addiction, when I had newly inflicted burns on my arms at every moment, I lived in a constant state of fear of people finding out. Accordingly, I spent most of my time alone.

As any addiction will do, self-injury caught up with me, and eventually it backfired. I began losing time from work and academic obligations, and I started having more severe and blackout episodes. The time spent obsessing and obsessing when trying to fight off that intense craving that comes before an oncoming episode, and the time spent coming down (much like "crashing" from a cocaine or amphetamine overdose), became a vicious cycle. The syndrome started to take control of my life. I started to have to leave classes and the workplace frequently, to "escape" to desperately find a place to self-injure. I would find such places as fire escapes and the local delis and fast-food restaurants like Jack in the Box that had one-person restrooms, where no one could hear me scream.

I was, however, always searching for solutions and trying to understand this thing because no one else did—not even the professionals I sought help from.

How I Recovered

I recovered from self-injury through the Twelve Step programs, having come to an understanding of the self-injurious behavior syndrome as an addiction and being able to identify as an addict. Traditional therapy was also helpful at various times as needed.

Being successfully in recovery and completely abstinent from self-destructive behaviors for more than seven years at the time of this writing, I am now able to share both my experience and knowledge in a more general way. My intent is to offer hope, understanding, and solutions to others.

Shortly after completing my doctorate, I was offered a post-doctoral fellowship in clinical psychology with a specialization in addictions at a major university medical school. I was not particularly interested in accepting because my main area of focus has been working with abused children, and this was working with adults only. But because I'm a strong advocate of family therapy in working clinically with children and teenagers, I figured that this would be beneficial in that I would learn more about how to help the kids' parents (many abused children do have an alcoholic or drug-addicted parent or stepparent in the picture).

When I accepted the fellowship, I was not yet in recovery. At the time, I was cutting and burning my arms about once a week, sometimes once every other week. I mistakenly thought that the self-injury problem would go away on its own. Things would be different, for sure, because work would take up every moment of my life. I quickly found out that becoming a workaholic did not work.

Quite to my surprise at that time, I found that many professionals working in the field of addictions happened to be recovering alcoholics or addicts themselves. These are the people who are best able to help alcoholics and addicts, since they come from a place of true understanding. Many are strong advocates of Twelve Step programs such as Alcoholics Anonymous (AA), Narcotics Anonymous (NA), and Cocaine Anonymous (CA). I saw how it worked for them, and how happy they seemed. They were able to handle life's challenges and difficulties very well while maintaining their recovery. I saw how it worked for the patients. What really impressed me was "the look in their eyes" of those truly committed to recovery. There is a sense of undisturbable peace of mind and calm and something genuinely spiritual that shines like a light from deep within the soul.

I began to theorize at that time about self-injury as an addiction and to attend Twelve Step meetings of any type, including Al-Anon, AA, and NA, that were open and accepting.

Even though my addiction was not to alcohol or drugs, something felt very right about this approach. Along the way, I met several other people who were also addressing their problems with self-injury in the Twelve Step meetings, either as their primary addiction or along with alcohol, drug addiction, eating disorders, and/or codependency.

I was fumbling around with going to meetings and not going to meetings for about a year and a half, doing the program half-heartedly because I was always "too busy." I would get a few weeks or a couple of months of abstinence together and then relapse again and again.

After one final episode that almost did me in (which was never my intention; I only wanted to escape from the emotional pain), I made the *commitment* to recovery. For me, my moment of commitment was a most sincere, heartfelt promise to God that I would stop hurting myself, with His help, after realizing and finally admitting to myself that my problem with self-injury was way out of control.

From that point on, I began to attend meetings faithfully, and still do, and to work the program and the Twelve Steps wholeheartedly. I always put my spirituality, which for me involves trusting God and helping others, first. Without that, I know that I would not have the wonderful, useful, and meaningful life that I have today.

Of everything I have accomplished in my life, of all my degrees, awards, and so on, the one thing that I am the most proud of and value the most is my *recovery* from self-injury. What I regret is the fact that I did not stop sooner— there are scars on my arms that will never heal, and so much time has been lost for me in terms of what could have been.

To those readers who are still struggling with the problem of self-injury, please make a *commitment* to stop hurting yourself now. Get professional help as soon as possible.

Don't go through this alone; you don't have to. I can promise you that you will have a much better and happier life if you stop this behavior and make a commitment to your recovery and stick with it. Even though it may seem hard at first, it does keep getting better. I know this from personal experience.

In the following pages you will learn more about how I successfully recovered and what treatment options might work for *you*. You will also hear about other people, both teenagers and adults, and things that have helped them. For instance, you will hear about how Patty, a thirteen-year-old girl with a long history of childhood sexual abuse and subsequent episodic cutting and burning, involvement in the teen Gothic scene, and alcohol and drug experimentation, did a lot to help herself while in a residential treatment program. If one treatment option doesn't work for you, don't give up. Keep trying other treatment options or a combination of various options.

Self-injury is never okay, not even one time. It's not okay even if you think that what you do to hurt yourself is "not all that bad." No one ever plans on becoming an alcoholic or an addict—it just sort of sneaks up and catches up with the person. Be sure to take care of the physical, emotional, and spiritual side of your life—it's all very important. And remember to stay focused on getting out of the problem and into the solution!

PART ONE

What Self-Injury Is All About

CHAPTER ONE

What Is Self-Injury?

~ ~ ~

That's it? "Bye" he just hung up and said "Bye" like, so cold, so businesslike ... Why doesn't he notice me, know I exist? I'm the one who's helping him so he won't flunk math class, it's just that I don't look like that bimbo over there. He had lunch with her the other day; it's just 'cause of her big knockers but she has a snot-face attitude and is mean to people, but I don't look like her so I'm worthless ...

They didn't notice me back in junior high; those boys were so mean when I was anorexic. I don't look like that now but still not good enough.

The racing thoughts

I can't slow down

My mom told me, "You're not good enough!" She beat me up when I got the first word wrong out of ten on a spelling test in first grade, just because it was the first one. Dad just stood there (why did he just stand there?); ignoring me, drinking whiskey out of coffee mugs with his dinner, pretending not to be an alcoholic, 'cause Italian Catholic fathers can do no wrong. Hey! Wait a minute! I still got an "A" and the nun gave me a gold star and a Virgin Mary sticker ...

Racing thoughts

I can't slow down

"I hate you! How could you get the first one wrong? The first one! What's wrong with you?"

Never good enough. It's never enough, never enough; I'm worthless.

He just said "Bye" and hung up the phone.

OH MY GOD, I'VE GOT TO GET MY HOMEWORK DONE AND I'M RUNNING OUT OF TIME, THERE'S NEVER ENOUGH TIME, I'VE GOT TO GET FOCUSED.

Looked over at the Oriental rug, out the beautiful Boston bay windows with the overpriced lace curtains, this house looks like the front of a Christmas card. Looked at the cold, dark, gray, hopeless sky in the middle of a cold, dark, gray, hopeless never-ending Boston winter.

(The pain never ends)

Spacing out

Numb

Waiting for the phone to ring again 'cause Andrew might call (but I know he won't). Who does he think he is? Thinking he's "all it" at the dance, flipping his hair back . . .

Looked down at his name carved across my leg over a month ago, A-N-D-R-E-W (why does he have to have such a long friggin' name?). That was stupid that I wrote his name, really deep and it won't go away, never even went out with him, hardly ever even talked with him, except for sitting next to him in math class. He doesn't even know I exist.

There's too much pain, too much heartache . . .

Turned up the stereo to drown out the pain. (But can't keep it on too long 'cause it's getting late and it might disturb Mrs. Grumbles, the old lady who lives next door.)

The thoughts just racing

Around and around

I'VE GOT TO GET MY HOMEWORK DONE

Numbing

Spacing out

I want my mom, but she's dead, been dead a long time. Forever. I want to cry but I can't. If I could just cry, I could, like, maybe slow down, but I can't think about that, 'cause if I break down, I'll never stop crying . . .

GOT TO GET MY HOMEWORK DONE, GOT TO GET FOCUSED

Looked over at the stove, the electric stove, the burners that will slowly turn bright

RED

I turned on the stove

(There's no turning back now)

Grabbed a metal spoon

("I'm into heavy metal now, just plain cutting doesn't work anymore")

Burned my upper arm

Where I usually do it

Where no one else can see

Over and over

Twice

And I still can't feel anything

Three times

Maybe more

Oh, my God, I just can't feel anything

I'm getting scared

Can't feel anything

It's not working anymore

Looked down at my leg

A-N-D-R-E-W

Took the spoon and burned over the dork's name

Left it there too long, way too long, 'cause I just can't feel anything

I heard my skin burn

And finally the welcome pain

Waiting for the relief
No, not this time
Only terror . . .
Heard the train, the sound of the oncoming train
But there was no train, the subway station is far away,
what is this train that I hear?
Heart racing, pounding
Thought I was gonna have a heart attack and die
(Please, God, I don't want to die. Please give me a
chance and I'll do things right. I promise I'll stop. I'll be good.
Know this is wrong. It's so wrong to destroy myself this
way . . .)
Ran to the bathroom
Looked in the mirror
My eyes were wired
Looked like I was on drugs, man
Speeding
Like on a speeding train without no brakes
Terror
Please, God, don't let me have a heart attack
Is this what happens when people have a heart attack?
Is this a stroke?
Looked in the mirror
I didn't recognize me
Didn't look like Veronica
Collapsed on the Oriental rug
Woke up minutes later or maybe hours later, who
knows . . .
It must have been a while. It's morning, the cat's hungry,
she's meowing . . .
Can't do this no more
It's over
It doesn't work anymore

∾   ∾   ∾

That was Veronica's final episode of self-injury, the one that led to her recovery. The racing thoughts that Veronica struggled with are typical for self-injurers. She is one of the fortunate ones who made a *commitment* to recovery—and who has been successfully maintaining recovery for many years—after having hit rock bottom. Today, Veronica is a very successful professional woman, who often states that "peace of mind" is one of the things she is most grateful for.

Defining Self-Injury

What exactly is the self-injurious behavior syndrome? It is the deliberate mutilation of one's own body, with the intent to cause injury or damage, but without intent to kill oneself. The self-injurer typically experiences an overwhelming impulse, for instance, to cut or burn herself, in conjunction with an increasing (escalating) sense of tension. This is followed by psychic relief ("Oh, I feel so much better!") after the injury is completed.

This problem, or disorder, typically begins in adolescence and continues over many years. As with other addictive disorders, there are repetitive episodes, with patterns of increasing frequency and severity, as time goes on.

What goes on in the mind of the self-injurer? In 1983, Pattison and Kahan wrote about the emotional and psychological side of self-injury. These authors describe the emotional/psychological symptoms frequently seen in self-injurers:

1. Sudden and recurrent intrusive impulses to hurt oneself, without the perceived ability to resist
2. A sense of being "trapped" in an intolerable situation that one can neither cope with nor control
3. An increasing sense of agitation, anxiety, and anger

4. When in this state, a constricted ability to "problem-solve," or to think of reasonable alternatives for action
5. A sense of psychic relief after the act of self-harm
6. A depressive or agitated-depressive mood, although suicidal ideation is not typically present

Why Self-Injury?

"Why would anyone want to hurt themselves on purpose? Well, if they did, it was probably just an accident . . ."

It happens, and a lot more often than one would dare to imagine. However, because the problem of deliberate self-harm, self-injury, self-mutilation, self-cutting, or self-injurious behavior syndrome is not yet well understood, many people—including parents, therapists, and other trained professionals—tend to avoid dealing with the issue. It is many times dealt with ineffectively. Most people tend to panic and "react" instead of respond or sometimes altogether dismiss the problem. The best way to understand what this disorder is—and what it is not—is to see how it affects the lives of people who have it.

Much like a person may use alcohol or drugs, or indulge in other self-destructive behaviors like anorexia or bulimia, one who self-injures is trying to run away from or "turn off" intolerable emotions and/or memories. Or to gain some sense of control.

∿   ∿   ∿

Sometimes, a person's inner pain and rage and frustration are so deep, so unbearable, that there are no words to describe the raging tornado building within her mind and body. An upsetting event happens; an unkind word is said; the sound of the wind chimes in the background trigger a memory of that summer at her grandmother's house in the country where her uncle molested her when she was five years old. Maybe nothing in particular happens; it's just been an annoying couple of days, and the broken shoelace, with no time left before having to catch the school bus, is the "straw that broke the camel's back." No words for oneself, let alone anyone else. An internal dialogue comes on, like a fast-moving train, usually in the abstract, obsessing and obsessing in images and sensations that seem to speak "to cut or not to cut, to cut or not to cut, to cut or not to cut …" The decision is made. An initial glimmer of relief, but there's more … in a split second or less, there are no more emotions, no more hurt feelings, just a sense of complete and total numbness. "Spacing out," much like daydreaming in a boring eighth-grade math class, but more … losing a sense of time, or of existing, or of being for real.… The knife touches the forearm, but no pain is felt, only a barely perceptive initial pinprick, followed by an awesomely numb sensation, much like the dentist's needle when you're getting Novocain. The knife runs deep, deep enough to finally draw blood, reality comes back, the colors and sensations in the room all get very bright and very strong, then finally the welcome pain, the scream, the relief, and it's over … for now.

~ ~ ~

What It Is and What It Isn't

As with any psychological concept or disorder that is not yet fully understood and that is just beginning to reach people's attention, there is a tendency to over-diagnose and to incorrectly diagnose self-injury. Some people think they see it everywhere—as with attention deficit disorder (ADD), many parents, teachers, professionals, and others would label a kid with ADD just because he jumped up and down a few times. Diagnoses must be made with caution, with understanding, and with respect to the individual.

Once when I was discussing my clinical work with self-injury, someone asked me, "My hairdresser has a lot of tattoos—do you think he has it?" It's possible but not likely. The popular "fads" of today, including tattoos and body piercing, may be just that—fads. Teenagers especially and very young adults may want to look "different" or "cool," or to make a statement, or to fit in with a particular group of friends.

The teenagers I have worked with in residential treatment centers and group homes are told the consequences for getting tattoos and body piercing such as nose rings and eyebrow rings. Their caretakers and counselors are concerned about risk of infection and HIV from dirty needles, as well as their displaying a look or image that their future employers may perceive as negative or gang-affiliated.

It's when a behavior is taken to an extreme, like anything else, that it becomes unhealthy and potentially dangerous. To determine whether tattooing and body piercing cross over the line into what is self-injury, a parent or professional may consider the following questions:

1. Is this behavior taken to an extreme?
2. Is this behavior compulsive?
3. Is the person becoming obsessed with the behavior?
4. Is the person craving the experience of pain?
5. Are there signs of self-inflicted wounds, such as cuts or burns?

If you answered "yes" to any of these questions, it is time to refer for help and address the problem.

Keep in mind that sometimes a person may have an isolated incident or a few incidents of self-injury that are merely for the purpose of getting attention. The behavior does not always become addictive. One social worker told me about an adult client of hers, Suzie, who happened to have a classic case of borderline personality disorder. Suzie cut her arm and strategically placed the drops of blood on a glass coffee table in the living room when she got mad at her boyfriend. This was a single incident, and the cut was minimal. The behavior was clearly manipulative and attention-getting, not the behavior of a person with the self-injurious behavior syndrome.

Most frequent methods of deliberate self-injury include

- cutting the skin with a knife or razor blade
- burning (for example, with a lit cigarette or heated metal)
- scratching the skin with fingernails (for example, scratching the skin hard enough to draw blood when in an escalated rage, not merely scratching a mosquito bite)
- biting oneself, including extreme episodes of nail-biting
- interfering with the healing of wounds (for example, compulsively picking at scabs)
- scalding hot showers
- head banging

In more severe cases, methods may include

- the breaking of bones
- amputation of fingers, limbs, or other body parts
- eye removal (enucleation)
- ingesting sharp or toxic objects (for example, razor blades, pins, cleaning fluids)

Secrets, Silence, and Shame

Self-inflicted injuries are typically superficial and, at most, may cause some minor scarring. However, sometimes an accidental slip of the razor blade or knife may cause a more serious injury. One may require medical care, such as stitches, or a visit to a hospital emergency room. When accidental injuries happen, the person may create a cover-up story for hospital personnel. Or, she may altogether refuse treatment, because she fears being "found out."

Denise, a seventeen-year-old who was also suffering with a severe case of bulimia, at one time gashed her leg in the high school bathroom with a razor blade. She had usually been scratching herself with a plastic comb "because it was there," but one morning before catching the school bus, she took one of her father's razor blades and threw it into her backpack. The incident happened when she was angry at her teacher, who she said "ignored her." The cut was more than she intended, because she was used to scratching herself with a comb, not a razor blade. When asked why she didn't get stitches, Denise replied, "I don't know."

There is also a great sense of shame, social stigma, and sometimes guilt associated with acts of self-harm. Therefore, the person usually attempts to hide scars, blood, or other "incriminating evidence." Frequently, a teenager who self-cuts will wear loose or baggy clothes and will always wear long sleeves, even in the summer. There can always be a clever excuse or rationale, for example, "It's my boyfriend's jacket; it has sentimental value." There may be frequent trips to the bathroom, either to self-injure or to attempt escape while trying to calm down and de-escalate when tension is mounting. To cover up, the self-injurer may create excuses such as, "Oh, I have a weak bladder; I drink a lot of water." Similar to bulimics who often hide their secret from others for months or years, those who suffer with the self-injurious behavior syndrome may also be able to hide their silent addiction from others for a long, long time.

So Misunderstood, Yet So Intriguing

The self-injurious behavior syndrome is not yet well understood and is alarming to many (probably most) people. This includes well-trained medical and mental health professionals. Anorexia and bulimia were just as shocking more than twenty years ago.

Today we have a much more comprehensive knowledge base about anorexia and bulimia. This is due to medical and psychological case studies, research, and circulation of knowledge to the public through books, articles, and the media. Furthermore, there are various different theories and points of view, as well as a number of available treatment options to choose from. Most people have at least heard about anorexia and bulimia, and they probably know of someone affected by it.

People who self-injure and are looking for help may run into brick walls over and over again when trying to find a therapist or anyone who is willing or able to effectively work with them. Sometimes, self-destructive behavior is mistakenly seen as suicidal behavior and thus treated incorrectly with inappropriate medical and psychotherapeutic inter ventions. If cuts are discovered on a self-injurer, she may be put into a hospital on a psychiatric unit because it is mistakenly thought that she tried to kill herself. Typically, she is released within a few days and feels more misunderstood and alone than ever. The cycle continues. . . .

Armando Favazza, a well-known medical doctor and researcher who has worked with and written about self-injurers, stated in 1988 that some chronic self-mutilators already are frequent and generally dissatisfied users of mental health services. Chronic self-mutilators present a true "blood and guts" therapeutic challenge. They are prone to recurrent crises and extreme sensitivity to rejection. The ever-present possibility of accidental suicide is there. This often creates feelings in therapists of anger, of helplessness, of pessimism, and of being torn apart and emotionally blackmailed.

It is therefore important that mental health and medical professionals as well as those who work with adolescents, such as schoolteachers, guidance counselors, and other school personnel, and parents become *educated*. Furthermore, there is a need for professionals especially to become *desensitized* to the blood-and-guts aspect of this disorder. They also need to be aware of and effectively handle the uncomfortable emotions that may arise in themselves in the role of helper or caregiver, emotions such as fear, helplessness, pessimism, and panic. When dealing with one who self-injures, the helper or caregiver needs to be able to, at least for the moment during times of crisis, not think about or focus on his or her own uncomfortable or nonfunctional emotions, much like an emergency room technician. The key is to respond instead of react.

Addicted to Pain

The self-injurious behavior syndrome should be seen as well as treated as an addiction. It may be the root to understanding all other addictions. According to *Webster's Dictionary, addict* is "to devote or surrender (oneself) to something habitually or obsessively (*addicted* to gambling)." *Addiction* is "compulsive need for and use of a habit-forming substance (as heroin)."

Addictions can be categorized as the following:

1. Alcohol and drug addictions, which involve the deliberate ingesting of a substance such as alcohol, cocaine, or heroin.
2. Behavioral addictions, which involve compulsive acts and obsessive thought processes. Certain behav-

ioral addictions may also involve significant physiological components, such as in anorexia, bulimia,
compulsive overeating, compulsive exercising, and
self-injury.

One who self-injures typically engages in a behavior that
is habit forming and that takes on an all-encompassing obsessional quality, with repetitive incidents of increasing frequency and severity. Research evidence, most notably the
work of Harvard psychiatrist Bessel van der Kolk and his
colleagues, suggests that self-injury causes a release of chemicals in the brain that are similar to addictive opiates. Therefore, it may be very difficult for a person who self-injures, once
"hooked," to simply just stop.

There is a strong correlation between self-injury and
other addictive behaviors. Many who self-injure also have
significant problems with alcohol, drugs, and/or eating disorders. Studies suggest that about 41 percent of bulimics
and 35 percent of anorexics also practice self-injury. It is
also known that repetitive acts of vomiting (as in bulimia)
cause the release of endorphins in the brain and may lead
to a physiologically addictive process. In self-injury, the
same type of "high" or physiological release is sought, although this is usually on a subconscious level.

As with other addictions, some treatment options seem
to work better for some people than for others. (Treatment
options will be described in chapter 6.) Depending on the
severity of the addiction, some people may need more help,
such as inpatient hospitalization, than others.

There are many theories as to what exactly causes addiction. These range from theories of deficits in the "self" or
personality; unresolved childhood issues; spiritual deficits;
learned behaviors; peer pressure; genetic predisposition or
causation; or the "disease" model, the belief that addiction
is a disease like cancer or diabetes.

Likewise, there is not a definitive answer as to what causes the self-injurious behavior syndrome. As with alcoholism, drug abuse, and eating disorders, there is not just one cause, but many factors involved. Self-injury is initially a learned behavior that may become addictive. Self-injury is usually not learned by direct observation, but rather by picking up on subconscious cues in the environment. For example, a physically or sexually abused child may subconsciously learn that when someone inflicts pain on her physical body, she can "go away," or escape. Therefore, she herself can deliberately inflict pain on her body whenever she wants to escape again (for example, when something bad happens or when someone says something mean and hurtful).

Does This Describe You or Someone You Know?

The self-injurer is not "unique" or alone, although she may feel that way. Over the last several years a number of common characteristics have been identified through clinical observations, case studies, and in contributions to the literature on self-injury. The three following lists of questions are a compilation of these. Questions relate to experiences, attributes, behaviors, and descriptive self-statements that tend to be prevalent among those who self-injure.

The self-injurer, especially one who is having a serious problem, will most likely be able to answer "yes" to many of the questions, especially on list 3. Because of the ambiguous and variable nature of the self-injurious behavior syndrome, there is not a set number of questions to be answered "yes" to or a specific pattern of symptoms that will apply to everyone. The purpose of these lists is to increase awareness.

The questions found in these lists can be used as a self-test, by and for the self-injurer. They can also be used by helping professionals or caregivers to gather more information about suspected self-injury.

Keep in mind that some people who do not self-injure will be able to relate to a few items, especially on lists 1 and 2. This is not unusual. For example, just because someone had an alcoholic father or is a high achiever, or both, does not mean that she is a self-injurer or is likely to become one. No self-injurer is likely to relate to every item, even on list 3, but will likely be able to identify with many.

List 1: Common Childhood History and Background Factors of Those Who Self-Injure

Many self-injurers have had some of the following experiences in their backgrounds, such as childhood abuse and eating disorders. Consider the following questions.

1. Do you have an alcoholic father?
2. Were you sexually abused as a child?
3. Were you physically abused as a child?
4. Were you emotionally abused as a child?
5. Were you neglected as a child?
6. Have you experienced severe trauma?
7. Was your mother not there, or emotionally not available?
8. Do you have, or have you had, anorexia?
9. Do you have, or have you had, bulimia?
10. Are you, or were you ever, a compulsive overeater?
11. In your childhood, was there a focus on religious images (bleeding statues, crucifixion of Christ, gory images)?
12. In your childhood, was there a focus on religious ideas related to pain and suffering (for example, "God loves those whom He makes suffer")?

13. Did you experience a lack of affection, touching, and hugging from others who should have been there for you as a child?
14. Did you not play with toys or dolls much as a child— and if so, did you not know what to do with them (especially dolls)?
15. Did you learn to walk late, and/or were you kept confined and overprotected as a child?
16. Are you, or were you, an exceptionally good student in school?

If something on list 1, Common Childhood History and Background Factors of Those Who Self-Injure, is causing you emotional distress and/or problems in functioning (such as eating disorders or memories of childhood abuse), it is advisable to seek help.

List 2: Common Personality Characteristics Seen in Self-Injurers

Self-injurers tend to have many of the following personality characteristics and experiences. Can you relate?

1. Are you highly intelligent?
2. Are you a high-functioning person?
3. Are you *driven* in work output, exercise, etc.?
4. Do your energy levels vary: extremely high/extremely low?
5. Do you like to "work hard and play hard"—make up for lost time?
6. Regarding drugs, do you like stimulants, uppers (not tranquilizers, marijuana, etc.)?
7. Are you feminine outside and masculine inside?
8. Do you have sexual identity issues (for example, bisexuality)?

9. Do you have sexual problems?
10. Do you have sadomasochistic (S&M) fantasies and/or actual experiences?
11. Do you have a great sense of pride ("I'm tougher than life")?
12. Do you feel you have, or have other people said you have, a sense of secrecy ("I've got a secret")?
13. Do you have a sense of uniqueness?
14. Do you feel that you are not understood by your therapist?
15. Have you had multiple therapists?
16. Do you feel that therapy did not help (with your self-injury)?
17. Do you sometimes feel that you "need a lift"?
18. Do you not have any major psychopathology (not psychotic, not schizophrenic, etc.)?
19. Do most people see you as pretty much normal?
20. Have you had psychiatric hospitalization(s)?
21. Do you have attention-getting and/or attention-seeking behaviors?
22. Do you have "victim" personality aspects (for example, has anyone ever said that sometimes you portray yourself as the "poor little victim")?
23. Do you have a codependent personality?
24. Do other people, especially those close to you, sometimes get extremely annoyed with you, and you really don't know why or what you did?
25. Do you have a high sexual drive?
26. Are you aggressive?
27. Are you sometimes seen as demanding/pushy by others?
28. Do you engage in frequent masturbatory activities, even if you have a spouse/sexual partner?
29. Are you multiorgasmic?

30. Would you say that you're not a "touchy-feely" person (for example, you don't like for people, especially those that are not close to you, to touch you or hug you)?

31. Do you sometimes feel an extreme need to be held?

32. Do you sometimes have personal grooming problems (for example, don't shower or wash your hair regularly)?

33. Do you have body image problems (for example, see yourself as "fat" or "ugly")?

34. Are you self-conscious about touching your own body (for example, in the shower)?

35. Are you "visual" in a sometimes obsessive-compulsive sort of way (for example, a towel not straight on a towel rack or a friend's earring crooked irritates you)?

36. Have you ever felt the urge to hurt someone (for example, to slap or punch out the boss or teacher)?

37. Have you acted on physical aggression?

38. Do you often feel misunderstood by others?

39. Are you a high achiever?

40. Do you have extreme highs (for example, happy outbursts or screams of joy when you see someone you haven't seen for a long time)?

41. Have you, or do you now, sometimes wear inappropriately revealing clothing, or portray an inappropriately sexy/flirtatious personal appearance?

42. Are you the dominant person in most interpersonal relationships?

43. Did your parents have hypochondriac/physical ailments or actual physical problems?

44. Do you have hypochondriac/physical ailments or actual physical problems?

45. Do you like to drive fast (whether or not you actually do, because of speeding laws)?

46. Have you had "psychic" or other premonition experiences?
47. Are your feelings/gut instincts very strong, and have you felt very sure of them, and have they been surprisingly accurate?
48. Are you very perceptive?

Items on list 2, Common Personality Characteristics Seen in Self-Injurers, are usually not of serious clinical concern, unless taken to an extreme (for example, aggressiveness or codependent personality). If there is a problem, seek professional help.

List 3: Self-Injury Checklist

The following is a list of common experiences, feelings, and self-statements made by self-injurers. Do these symptoms sound familiar to you?

1. Do you have more than one method of self-injury (cutting, burning, etc.)?
2. Do you have problems with dissociation (for example, "spacing out," feeling like you're not really there)?
3. Do you not feel pain while self-injuring?
4. Do you self-injure alone (it's not a party thing)?
5. Have you found in your experience that self-injury breeds in confinement (institutions, group homes, etc.)?
6. Do you wear long sleeves and clothing that covers/hides a lot in the summer?
7. Do you sometimes feel that you need to be "put back to reset"?
8. Do you sometimes feel that you're at the point of being "too far gone" (for example, that you're going to hurt yourself no matter what)?

9. Do you sometimes feel that you are in a point of dilemma/internal conflict: "to cut or not to cut?"
10. Do you have a feeling of relief: "it's over" after the self-injury?
11. Are you visual regarding the self-injury: do you need to see blood, burn mark, etc.?
12. Do you ever feel emotionally numb?
13. Do you have states of extreme anger or agitation?
14. Do you have states of emotional escalation, especially regarding anxiety?
15. Do you have the feeling of "I know what I'm doing"— of being in *control* when doing the self-injury?
16. Are friends/people surprised when they find out you self-injure?
17. Do you have control issues? (Many times self-injury happens when you feel that you've lost control over a situation.)
18. Do trivial incidents sometimes seem to drive you over the edge—for example, something minor like a broken shoelace with no time left to fix it can be "the straw that broke the camel's back"?
19. Are you sometimes really angry at another person when you self-injure?
20. Do you ever feel that self-injury is the only thing that doesn't infringe on another person or another person's rights—it's better than drunk driving?
21. Do you have a feeling of release, like sexual orgasmic experience (but not sexual in nature) that results from the self-injury?
22. Is your self-injury superficial and without suicidal intent?
23. Have other people (such as mental health professionals) sometimes misunderstood self-injurious behaviors as suicidal attempts/ideation?

24. Do you feel that you can't hurt yourself unless "in that state"?
25. Do you feel that although there are some things you do, there are some methods of self-injury that you don't do that just wouldn't do anything for you (for example, fork swallowing or eye removal) that others use to get the same type of high?
26. Do you not let scars heal (compulsively pick at scabs, etc.)?
27. Have you tried various methods yourself to try to stop self-injuring (putting your hand in an ice bucket, calling a friend, etc.)?
28. Are there some times when one or some of these things might work (and you actually stop the escalating and don't hurt yourself) but other times when nothing works?
29. Do you get a "high" from the self-injury experience?
30. Are your scars, and burn marks especially, strategically placed (for example, purposefully placed on certain specific locations of your arm or leg)?
31. Do you spend a lot of time alone?

If you (or someone you know) can identify with items on list 3, Self-Injury Checklist, it is time to seek help. These are common in people who are struggling with a serious problem of self-injury.

CHAPTER TWO

Why an "Addiction"?

Clinical and research literature as well as popular textbooks on self-injury have at times alluded to, in a vague sort of way, the fact that self-injury is "like" an addiction. However, this theoretical framework and approach to treatment, of viewing self-injury from an addictions perspective, has not yet been fully explained or developed.

Throughout this book, self-injury is explained from an addictions perspective. Explanations, approaches to treatment, and case examples not only of self-injurers but also of alcoholics, drugs addicts, and those who are multi-addicted are woven throughout this book to illustrate the addictive process and the similarities across addictions.

This chapter contains some technical terms and complex concepts. The book is intended primarily as a resource for people who have the problem of self-injury and for the people in their lives who care, which includes medical and mental health professionals. Some readers may wish to skim or skip over the more technical sections on *DSM-IV* clinical diagnostic criteria and biochemical theories. Feel free to do so if you like, and move on to other sections of the book that you can relate to.

There is no clear-cut, simple definition of addiction that I have found to be quite satisfactory. A simplistic definition cannot account for all of the signs and symptoms of the addictive process. However, a person can be reliably classified as an addict based on different combinations of basic characteristics. Most addicts show only certain combinations. Coupled with the addict's characteristic strong denial system, diagnosis can at times be difficult, unless the addiction is severe or obviously brought to attention.

The most meaningful conception of addiction that I have found is one that was developed by Chein and his colleagues from a study of heroin addicts in New York City. Their book *The Road to H* (1964) is considered a classic. Their description of the addictive process experienced by heroin addicts extends to other addictions as well. It supports the generality of all addictions, including that of self-injury.

As shown in the "Chein criteria" below, there are most striking similarities between heroin addicts and self-injurers. Heroin is an opioid addiction, and self-injurers produce their own internal opioids through a subconscious physiological process, to which they can become addicted. Hence, this is a highly applicable and a particularly useful conception for our purposes.

The Chein criteria are

1. physical dependency
2. craving
3. total personal involvement

Physical dependency involves a history of repeated episodes that lead to some sort of intoxication (for example, getting drunk or high). It does not apply to being intoxicated only one time. There is a need for a larger dose of the drug (or a greater intensity of the self-injurious act—for example, progressing from delicate self-cutting on to burning) as time goes by, to produce the same effect. This is called tolerance.

Connie, a twenty-five-year-old graduate student, who had

progressed from scratching and cutting to deep burning, would experience an extreme "high" from her self-injurious behavior. It scared her when a roommate (who herself was in and out of treatment for cocaine and alcohol abuse) once stated: "Girl, I've never seen anyone get as high as you do (when you hurt yourself) from no matter what kind of alcohol, drugs, cocaine, or anything else—and I've seen it all and done it all myself—you better be careful! Someday you're going to have a heart attack or stroke and die!" Still, she could not stop.

Cross-tolerance may occur and will often happen within the same class of drugs. For instance, under the sedative/hypnotic category, people may show cross-tolerance to alcohol and barbiturates. Connie, like many other self-injurers, also had an ongoing problem with substance abuse. Her drugs of choice were cocaine and uppers "to bring my mood up when I'm down."

Addicts who are not only psychologically but also physically addicted may experience physical withdrawal symptoms when not using for a critical period of time. This may include nausea, shaking, sweating, and sometimes even convulsions and hallucinations in severe cases. Because both heroin and the internal physiological changes that occur in self-injury are powerful analgesics (chemicals that cause insensitivity to pain), these types of addicts are, to varying degrees, unfamiliar with physical and emotional pain. So, they become terrified of withdrawal (and the resulting feelings that come to surface), especially during detoxification. This is why many heroin addicts move on to methadone maintenance, a much safer form of the drug that produces some of the same desired effects. These addicts may visit methadone maintenance clinics on a regular basis, sometimes indefinitely. Likewise, self-injurers sometimes choose a safer alternative, for example, medically prescribed psychotropic medication such as antidepressants. Some addicts may decide to avoid withdrawal at all costs.

Craving is defined by Chein and his associates as (1) an "abnormal intensity of desire," (2) an extreme reaction to failure to satisfy the desire, and (3) an abnormal limitation in the modifiability of the desire.

Craving involves an all-encompassing obsession or preoccupation. Some addicts will go to any lengths to obtain a drug. Stories of addicts who steal money or hock possessions that belong to their own parents or who break into pharmacies or go directly to bars immediately after being released from jail or treatment centers are quite common. When self-injury addicts have an intense craving, they may go to any lengths to find places to hide to indulge in their self-destructive behavior. They may find things that they can hurt themselves with even in locked institutions where all dangerous objects have presumably been removed.

Clarice, a thirteen-year-old girl from Philadelphia, was taken to a small, private general psychiatric hospital by her parents. They were at wit's end with her compulsive, repetitive self-injurious behavior. She came in with her (much older and drug-involved) boyfriend's name slashed across her arm, bragging about it to the other teenagers on the young people's unit. Hospital staff searched Clarice's bags and took all sharp implements away from her upon entry, including the safety pins that she used to hold up her favorite jeans with the broken zipper. It particularly bothered her that she had to ask staff every time she needed a pencil to do her homework, which she hated doing anyway. One day when Clarice became frustrated, she managed to break and use a lightbulb in her room to cut herself. Subsequently, she was moved to the front hallway by the nurse's station, where the kids with medically complicated cases could be more closely observed. Most of the staff's attention at the time was on the girl in the room next to her. Lisa, a seventeen-year-old beauty queen who was diabetic, had to take insulin injections every day and was detoxing from a variety of street drugs. One evening when Clarice was having an intimate conversation with one of her favorite nurses, Lisa had a medical episode. The nurse had to get up and leave the conversation and run to Lisa's aid, which made Clarice very angry. She emotionally escalated. Frantically searching around the room for something to hurt herself with, she spotted the flower arrangement her aunt had sent her, on the dresser. She managed to create a sharp enough instrument by unwrapping and twisting together several of the very thin green-paper-wrapped wires used to hold the pink carnations in place. This and another bloody arm-scratching episode all happened while sitting on the bed under a blanket, pretending to be reading an English book. When later discovered, Clarice was terminated from the hospital program.

No matter what happens, the severe addict continues to use and abuse despite the consequences of her addiction.

A pattern of *total personal involvement* with drugs characterizes the lives of many addicts, according to Chein and his associates. This also applies to alcoholics in regard to their alcohol and to self-injurers in regard to their self-destructive behaviors. Total personal involvement means that the addict's personality structure is built around his or her addiction. Drugs, alcohol, or self-injury have become essential to the personality when (1) the person feels "normal" only when under the influence or (2) certain aspects of the personality are expressed only under the influence. For example, a cocaine addict may become self-confident, socially outgoing, and flirtatious around men only when she is high.

The Self-Medication Hypothesis

A number of researchers in the field of addictions have proposed that addicts who have a difficult time managing their affect (that is, have difficulty in bringing to order their conscious subjective experience of emotions) use alcohol or drugs as a way to self-medicate.

Khantzian (1985, 1990) described addiction as "a purposeful attempt by the addict to remediate a particular dysfunction." He noted that addicts who reported depression chose addictive substances that relieved the uncomfortable sad feelings and that addicts who did not have a normal level of feeling sensitivity chose addictive substances that stimulated them.

Other researchers have also studied and substantiated Khantzian's hypothesis that *specific drugs* were selected on the basis of the drug's particular ability to reduce unacceptable feelings or to amend unwanted emotional states. Cocaine and amphetamines were selected by addicts who sought more stimulation. Alcohol and opiates were preferred by those who wished to escape from intolerable emotions.

Researchers have also tested the idea that addicts' drugs of choice were based on their *particular defensive style.* Findings included, for example, that amphetamine addicts used stimulants because they wanted to experience an inflated sense of self-worth. Narcotics were used to defend against intolerable feelings of hurt, rage, shame, and loneliness.

Self-injurers use their addiction as a way to self-medicate, as alcoholics and other addicts often do. Deliberate self-injury can be either a method of stimulation to escape depression, numbness, and feeling "dead inside" or a method to relieve anxiety and agitation. Many self-injurers have used and are at a very high risk for using and abusing alcohol and other drugs. Some self-injurers may prefer drugs such as cocaine or amphetamines; some may prefer alcohol or heroin; and some may vary their choice of substance from time to time, depending on what uncomfortable emotional state they want to relieve.

Biochemical Theories: Trauma, Addiction, and Self-Injury

Research on biochemical theories and physiological explanations of self-injury is still in its beginning stages. There are not yet any final answers or definitive conclusions. However, we do know that self-injury involves both physiological and psychological processes. Much of the research and theorizing about the biochemical theories and physiological explanations regarding self-injury stem from the work on trauma and post-traumatic stress disorder (PTSD), because similar factors and processes are involved.

One of the common processes is stress-induced analgesia, or numbing. People with severe numbing almost always have PTSD. There is an interrelationship between trauma, particularly childhood trauma (child abuse), and self-injurious behavior and other addictions.

According to trauma expert John Briere, people with PTSD develop new avoidant strategies. These may include, for example, drugs, alcohol, self-mutilation, violence, and shoplifting. Briere explains self-mutilation as "a way to alter your affect." In an October 2000 seminar on complex psychological trauma and PTSD (in California), Briere cited a clinical example of a fourteen-year-old girl who described a "physical equivalent of cocaine" when running a paper clip over her arm and bleeding.

Cutting, burning, and other self-injurious behaviors may be a way to manage unbearable emotions by altering interpersonal conditions as well as by altering the body's biological balance. Bessel van der Kolk, M.D., and colleagues at Harvard Medical School (1991) have proposed that "the fact that both the severity of the trauma and the age at which it occurred affected the particular ways in which our subjects were self-destructive suggests that both psychological and biological maturity play a role in how experiences of abuse and neglect are managed."

There are a number of studies indicating that disruptions in early caregiving may have long-term consequences for biological self-regulating systems. The effects of trauma and early maternal and social deprivation have been extensively studied in animals. Research on nonhuman primates has demonstrated that self-mutilation is a common reaction to social isolation and fear. Experimental animals that have been exposed to inescapable stressors (for example, electric shock, fighting, and starvation) develop stress-induced analgesia (numbing). Fear activates the secretion of endogenous (internally produced) opioids, which can become highly addictive. In animals that have been severely stressed, withdrawal symptoms can be produced by stopping the stressful stimulus. (This explains from an addictions perspective why it is so difficult for severe self-mutilators to stop.)

In animals, harmful stimuli (reminders) continue to precipitate conditioned biological "emergency" responses over time, resulting in "fight, flight, or freeze" reactions. Younger, developmentally immature animals are especially vulnerable to developing these conditioned emergency responses to repeated stress. This holds true for abused children as well.

People who have endured severe trauma react, and continue to react, with extremes of underarousal or overarousal. They respond to stimuli (triggers) that remind them of the original trauma with conditioned psychological and biological stress responses. Current research on traumatized children has identified a wide range of neurobiological abnormalities in this population, and that children who have been victims of abuse have chronic problems with affect management, which range from extremes in hyperactivity to psychic numbing.

Self-injurers are prone to experience intense physiological disorganization as a result of repeated self-inflicted trauma on top of their already existing childhood abuse or other life trauma. Thus, they may follow similar psychological and biological response patterns as do the experimental animals that have been exposed to extreme stress.

Van der Kolk, Perry, and Herman (1991) found that two decades after the original trauma, people with post-traumatic stress disorder developed opioid-mediated analgesia (numbing) in response to a stimulus resembling the original traumatic stressor, which they correlated with a secretion of endogenous opioids equivalent to 8 mg of morphine. They concluded, "Dissociation, self-destructiveness, and impulsive behavior may all prove to be hormonally mediated responses that are triggered by reminders of earlier trauma and abandonment."

An Explanation, Not an Excuse

There is convincing evidence from a biological/physiological basis to describe the connection between trauma, self-injury, and addiction. There is a predominant theoretical view that these biological and physiological factors, internal wiring, and effects on the body's central nervous system are permanent. It is an explanation, but not an excuse to react by using alcohol, drugs, or self-injury to try to "fix" the problem.

What is important is that we respond effectively to what is, instead of reacting to whatever it is in a dysfunctional way. For those who have been traumatized, and for those with chemical imbalances or who are otherwise prone to alcoholism and other addictions (for example, due to genetic or familial factors), this can be extremely difficult. Self-medicating to get rid of the inner pain and turmoil is tempting.

The Vipassana method of meditation (*Doing Time, Doing Vipassana* 1997) is a method of reform that is widely taught and being used in the prison systems in India. Because of very positive results, it is starting to make its way to other places, including the United States. Before embarking on this voluntary educational experience, the prisoners are required to make a commitment to refrain from all use of alcohol and drugs, sexual behavior, and acts of violence, at least for the duration of the course, so that they can free themselves from external distractions. This ten-day intensive meditation course teaches people—namely, hardened criminals who have a history of violent behaviors and many of whom also have addictions—to learn to sit quietly with their emotions, flooding of memories and flashbacks, and accompanying physical sensations

The Vipassana view is that "The root to all our physical addictions and emotional reactions comes from our physical sensations within the body. And that one must learn to go inside, to sit with it, and to not react to these internal feelings."

Child physical abuse, sexual abuse, and trauma such as rape are unconscionable acts that are difficult for most anyone to comprehend. (See figure 1, page 42.) A very young child typically does not yet have the knowledge that these things *can* actually happen; it is out of her frame of reference. Being overpowered and trapped in the grip of her abuser, someone who is older and stronger, someone whom she looks up to, trusts, and is dependent on for her care and survival (for example, the abusive parent), is beyond the scope of what she can comprehend on an intellectual level, let

FIGURE 1.
ORIGINAL TRAUMA AND TRAUMATIC MEMORY PAIN REACTION

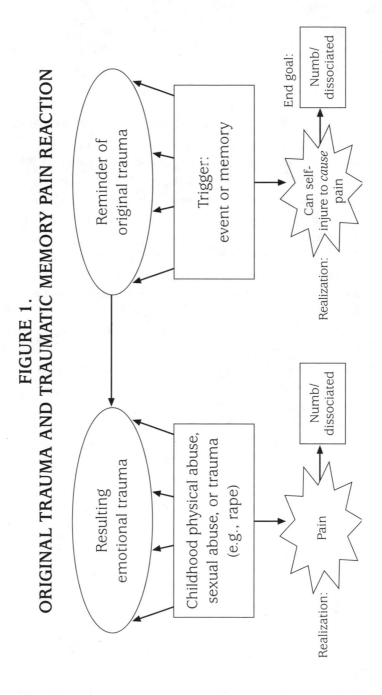

alone deal with on an emotional level. The resulting emotional trauma is too confusing and overwhelming, too much for her to deal with. Therefore, she becomes emotionally and physically numb, dead inside, and dissociates.

The traumatized child probably does not have the words, or may not even know enough words yet, to explain this to herself in her own mind or to anyone else. She is operating at a preverbal level, experiencing only vague floating thoughts, muffled sounds, physical sensations, and visual images. Being forced to undergo and endure violence at the hands of another person, being trapped with no way out . . . is utterly unbearable. The only place to go is within, or away.

However, the abused child's subconscious mind is hard at work during all this. The abused child who grows up to be a self-injurer makes the connection that physical pain itself is a way to escape. Not in so many words, but rather in thoughts and images, she figures out that "when pain happens, this means that I can go away. There is a way out!" This idea becomes reinforced in her mind, over and over, with the reoccurrence of the physical or sexual abuse. Verbal abuse, witnessing domestic violence, or seeing the erratic behavior of an alcoholic/addict parent, and other negative experiences that are emotionally overwhelming add to it. She can go away, or space out, or go off into dreamland anytime she becomes emotionally overwhelmed, and feel nothing instead. She learns how to become numb and to dissociate. She learns that she does not "really" have to experience anything she does not want to experience.

A newspaper article written by Tracy Weber in the *Los Angeles Times* (1998), entitled "Despair of the System Kids," spoke of one such teenage girl who had been repeatedly abused since she was a toddler. Jessica could not escape the violent environment and unfortunate circumstances that she was forced to endure. Sent back and forth between her drug-involved mother's home, being placed with an aunt, and shuffled around from group home to group home, Jessica felt "trapped."

Jessica had first come to the attention of county social workers when she was three years old, after her mother's boyfriend whipped her during a drug-fueled rage. There were several other incidents of domestic violence throughout her childhood, which brought the attention of the police in response to her mother's screams. Jessica was placed with an aunt at the age of eight while her mom kicked her methamphetamine habit. She was eventually returned home, but when she was ten, the mother's boyfriend's father reportedly sexually abused her during a camping trip. Jessica fought with her mother, to no avail. By twelve, she was a chronic runaway and had been placed in a psychiatric hospital twice. Her mother eventually drove her to the county's shelter for abused children, insisting that they take her daughter. By the age of fourteen, Jessica became a "system kid," being shuffled from one group home to another . . .

The newspaper article begins:

"Jessica's childhood is etched in shiny scar tissue. Each thin slash on her forearm is a memento of another stint in the county's home for abused kids. Each lumpy burn—a smiley face seared with the metal top of a disposable cigarette lighter—another group home that didn't work out. 'Some were because I wanted to make my mom feel bad,' Jessica says, 'Some were because my life sucks.'"

The original traumatic experience becomes imprinted in the subconscious memory of a self-injurer, and in physical sensations in her body, permanently. The body remembers what the mind does not.

As time goes on and the years go by, life happens, as it will . . . emotionally difficult experiences, negative situations, and daily frustrations are inevitable, for everyone in the world. However, such experiences seem to affect the self-injurer in a more profound way and thus cause her to react in the most effective, albeit destructive, way that she knows how.

Other experiences that are difficult to deal with on an emotional level, along with the uncomfortable feelings, remind her of the past. As the self-injuring episodes continue, the idea that "physical pain is a way to escape" becomes reinforced. She learns that this idea can be applied to cope with just about anything that is difficult or uncomfortable. This includes even the minor annoyances and daily hassles of life, such as a flat tire or a squabble with her boyfriend about what toppings to get on a pizza.

The originally traumatized child who grows up to be a self-injurer has found a faulty, yet effective, way to cope with life in general. The fact that self-injury is destructive and that it can be very dangerous are secondary or not important to her at all.

Anything can be an emotional trigger—an event, a memory, a childhood flashback, or a nightmare. A triggering event or memory reminds her of the original trauma (for example, the physical or sexual abuse) and/or the resulting suppressed emotional feelings that went along with it. Sometimes feelings such as frustration, anxiety, loss of control of a situation, or entrapment in and of themselves are enough to make one remember, even if these feelings are connected to some present, seemingly irrelevant or trivial situation. And to remember that there is a way to escape.

The self-injurer realizes, albeit on a subconscious level, that physical pain equals escape and ultimate freedom. And that she can cause herself to experience physical pain (with the end goal of going away and having no feelings) by hurting herself on purpose.

Understanding and becoming fully conscious of the dynamics involved, of both the original trauma and the resultant subconsciously ingrained and well-learned defective coping mechanisms used in the present, can help to break this cycle. Becoming verbal helps.

The Deliberate Self-Harm Escalation/De-escalation Cycle

According to the clinical, medical, and biochemical research literature, there are two very different main conclusions as to the reasons "why" people self-injure:

1. to escape by becoming emotionally numb and dissociating
2. to relieve states of escalated anxiety and agitation

Clinicians and researchers have not yet come up with a single definitive answer. This is likely because some self-injurers describe having either one or the other type of experience, which is true for them. Some self-injurers describe variable feelings and experiences, which are confusing to both themselves and to outsiders. They self-injure sometimes to become numb and dissociate, and other times to relieve feelings of anxiety and agitation.

The following figures describe the two different processes (see pages 47, 52). This information has been gathered and put together over years of clinical work with and observations of self-injurers and addicts, reading the research literature and numerous case histories, talking with other self-injurers, and understanding this from my own personal experience.

Some self-injurers who read this may have slightly different perceptions in regard to their specific experience. This is, however, a composite view of what is most general.

When an event or memory occurs that on some level

FIGURE 2.
PURPOSE: TO RELIEVE AND REPRODUCE NUMBNESS/DISSOCIATION

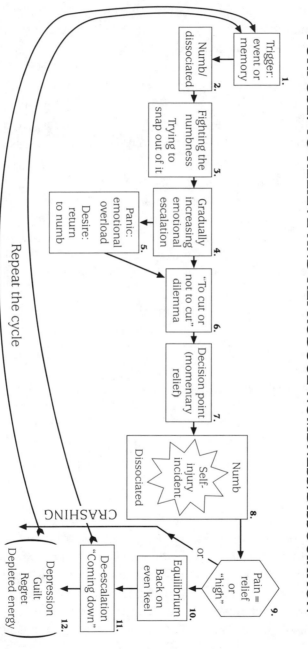

reminds the self-injurer of the original trauma or the resulting emotions attached to it (a "trigger"), the goal is to once
again become numb and dissociate, to go away. However,
the one who has been traumatized in the past eventually
becomes more aware of her environment, of the people
around her, of the fact that this behavior is socially inappropriate and frowned upon, and that self-injury can (at least
temporarily) impede her ability to function. Thus, a state of
internal conflict is born.

The serious self-injurer becomes caught in an addictive
cycle. A triggering event or memory happens, which causes
her to automatically become numb and dissociate. However, she will most likely try to "snap out of it," to fight the
numbness, much like someone pinches herself if she is
getting sleepy and groggy but has to stay awake while driving a car.

Next, the self-injurer becomes briefly aware of the reality
around her. A gradual sense of increasing emotional escalation occurs when thoughts and feelings begin to drift back.
Eventually, the self-injurer is on emotional overload; she
panics and has a desire to return to numb. This may happen
in a moment or over the course of days.

Hence the dilemma: "To cut or not to cut, to cut or not to
cut, to cut or not to cut." It is a horrible internal struggle of
an obsessive nature. This is very similar to what an alcoholic
or addict experiences when obsessing about drinking or
doing drugs.

Speaking from experience, the obsessional phase was,
for me, most intolerable. The thoughts of wanting and actually needing to hurt myself, knowing it was wrong, and trying futilely to talk myself out of it, became overwhelming
and distracting to the point where I could not concentrate,
especially when it went on too long. In the first three to five
months of my recovery, I had to learn to sit with those un-

comfortable thoughts, feelings, and physiological sensations continually, without even momentary relief, which was one of the hardest things I've ever had to do. I would never want to go back to that place again. There was no easy way out, but getting through it successfully made me a very strong person.

When the person reaches the decision point that she is going to hurt herself, she experiences a sense of momentary relief. However, it is only momentary. She may self-injure immediately or have a plan to do this later on, for example, after work when she has time to go to the drug store and get a six-pack of razor blades and a bottle of wine to go with it.

This sense of relief is similar to what suicidal people experience when they make the decision to kill themselves. People around them, sometimes even their therapists, think that the suicidal person is doing better now, that he or she seems a lot happier. Clinicians who work with self-injurers need to become aware of this.

Just before and throughout the self-injury incident, the self-injurer once again becomes numb and dissociated. She cannot, or will not want to, hurt herself unless she is in that state. This state comes on primarily on its own. However, she may use alcohol or drugs to help get her there faster or to intensify the experience. Mostly, she produces her own internal anesthetic within her mind and body. Then it happens.

During the self-injury incident, so much endorphin release occurs that one can get "high." There is a welcome sense of relief. Pain equals relief, or getting high. The experience of pain becomes addictive. The self-injurer comes to like pain, and she eventually craves it.

The self-injurer's mind and body then return to a state of balance, or equilibrium. She is back on an even keel, which for her means being at least somewhat high for a while, because her most usual state is one of feeling down and depressed.

Next, the self-injurer gradually de-escalates from the high, both physically and psychologically. She experiences a comfortable, physically and emotionally tolerable, level of pain. She may pick at the scabs or wounds as she is de-escalating, or coming down, to prolong the pleasant experience or to avoid withdrawal.

Finally, the inevitable depression, guilt, and regret come along. She feels even worse than she did before. Her physical and emotional energy are depleted. "Crashing" means coming down quickly and very hard. This feeling is similar to what happens with a major dose of certain drugs such as cocaine, amphetamines, or other stimulants.

She may get back on the self-injury roller coaster again and again. She may want to escape again, or to feel good, or to get high. Eventually, the experience becomes addictive. The self-injurer typically repeats the cycle either when she is de-escalating, or coming down, or when she is feeling depressed or her physical and psychological energy are depleted. She does not do this when she is feeling good, or back on an even keel, and simply enjoying and coping with life. When de-escalating or back to her usual depressive state, a triggering event or memory happens, as it inevitably will, that sets her off. The self-injury addict repeats the vicious cycle again. She may even look for or "create" a triggering situation to avoid withdrawal, by scanning the environment for something to get upset about (one can always find something!). Or worse yet, she may subconsciously deliberately put herself in negative or dangerous situations, such as picking fights and arguments with people, or becoming caught up in abusive relationships.

Many self-injurers describe feelings of escalating anxiety and agitation, frustration, anger, and rage that are utterly intolerable. These self-injurers are more visible to both clinical professionals and to the general public. Their self-injuring episodes are typically more severe and more dramatic. The injuries are more significant, possibly even life threatening, due to their impulsive nature. These self-injurers may appear as people who are more outspoken and always angry, agitated, frustrated, argumentative, loud and hyperactive, speeding around, and with dramatic up-and-down mood swings.

The following describes what happens when one self-injures for the primary purpose of relieving anxiety and agitation (see figure 3, page 52):

A triggering event or memory happens. The person "reacts" immediately, feeling anxious and agitated. These feelings escalate rapidly. One may appear to be emotionally overwhelmed, as if she is "speeding," with racing heart and frantic mannerisms. She may be crying and hyperventilating. Depending on how fast the escalation happens, how intolerable her emotions are, and how impulsive she is, the self-injurer may go either straight to the self-injury incident or through the process of a more gradual emotional escalation and become numb and dissociated before she hurts herself. This second process is similar to what has been described in figure 2, with a few variations: The emotional escalation is much more rapid; the goal of self-inflicted pain is primarily to become calm and "comfortably numb"; and the downfall to depression is much more rapid and severe.

With impulsive self-injury, one does not have time to numb out and dissociate or to even think about what she is doing. Impulsive behavior can be extremely dangerous.

FIGURE 3.
PURPOSE: TO RELIEVE ANXIETY/AGITATION

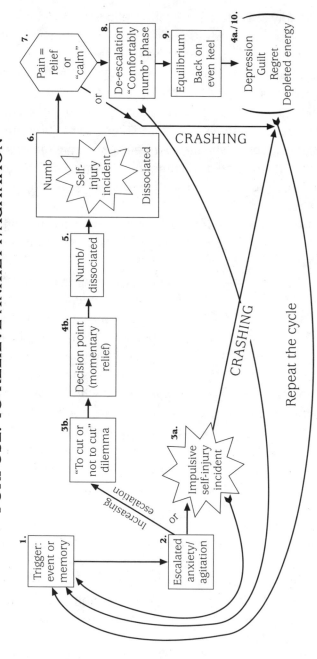

This is what happened to seventeen-year-old Denise in chapter 1, when she impulsively slashed her leg with a razor blade in her classroom, immediately without stopping to think or to breathe, because she got mad at her teacher.

With impulsive acts of self-injury, there is no great feeling of relief, maybe just a momentary but intense "high," or a brief feeling of calm. Equilibrium is not restored. The self-injurer crashes rapidly, falling down into depression-guilt-regret and exhausting her supply of energy. She may repeat the cycle when going down too low, because being emotionally escalated, anxious, and agitated is her more natural state of being. She wants to restore her status quo. However uncomfortable it may be, at least it is familiar. Or she may get back on the roller coaster when the "comfortably numb" feeling starts fading away.

Impulsive incidents of self-injury provide an answer to the frequently asked question: "Why do some self-injurers say that they feel pain and some say they don't while self-injuring?" Pure physical pain caused by an impulsive self-injury incident, that results in pure physical injury (for example, the breaking of bones or a burn) with no internally produced anesthetic, hurts like hell. It's like accidentally getting burned on an iron or a hot stove. Even with more thought-out and deliberate acts, the self-injurer may not become numb and dissociated enough to not feel the pain. It's like not having enough internally produced anesthetic to fit the experience. (See figure 4, page 54.)

However, many self-injurers, especially those whose afflictions are more severe and have been having repetitive episodes over a long period of time, have unintentionally "perfected" their ability to not feel pain. They have learned to avoid feeling acute severe physical pain in general. This can include subconsciously avoiding the beneficial physical

FIGURE 4. THE SELF-INJURER'S TYPICAL EXPERIENCE OF ACUTE VS. CHRONIC PAIN

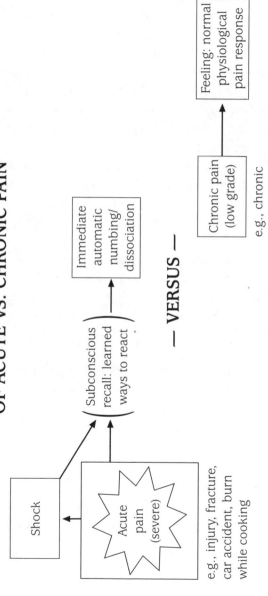

pain that occurs to alert us that there is an injury to or a malfunction in the body that needs tending to. Acute, severe pain—like from a fractured leg or a burn while cooking—"shocks" the self-injurer on an emotional level. This causes an immediate subconscious recall of the over-learned way to react. The experienced self-injurer, or even some young children who have been repeatedly physically or sexually abused, can immediately and seemingly automatically become numb and dissociate. Unfortunately, sometimes the numbing and dissociation goes on too long, and the self-injurer may not realize that she is seriously hurt or ill. Needless to say, if physical injuries or illnesses are not tended to, they can become significantly worse.

Chronic or low-grade pain is different. It does not shock the system and generally does not cause one to instantaneously react by becoming numb and dissociated. In this case, the person has feeling, a normal physiological pain response. It is uncomfortable, but tolerable. Chronic and low-grade pain may result from, for example, a chronic illness such as an arthritic condition, or from minor ailments such as headaches or menstrual cramps, or from physical injuries during the healing phase.

Withdrawal from a severe, repetitive pattern of self-injury, when one is addicted, has many characteristics in common with alcohol and drug withdrawal (see figure 5, page 56).

A severe self-injury incident occurs. (The self-injurer may or may not be numb/dissociated.) After the pain, the person comes "crashing" down and is physically and emotionally exhausted.

As with withdrawal from substances such as opiates, cocaine, alcohol, or amphetamines, the withdrawing self-injurer may experience a variety of psychologically distressing symptoms. These may include, for example, extreme

FIGURE 5. SELF-INJURY WITHDRAWAL

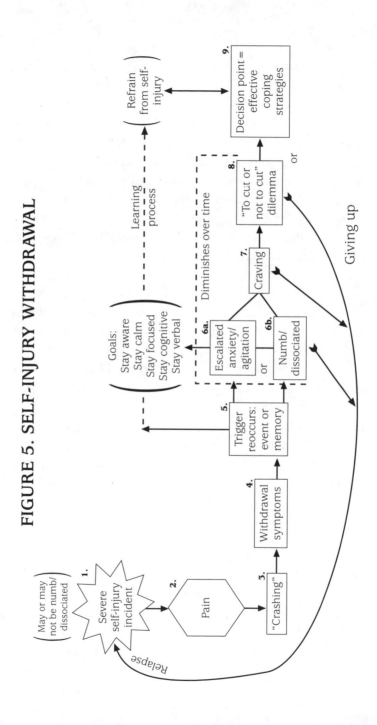

depression and/or anxiety. There may also be a sense of confusion and disorientation. The self-injurer may appear "spaced out" to others. Some self-injurers report experiencing fatigue, insomnia or hypersomnia (sleeping too much), muscle aches and pains, and vivid horrifying dreams or flashbacks after stopping their behavior. These symptoms steadily diminish in severity and duration as the addictive substance (the internally produced opiates) wear off. Such unpleasant symptoms can cause significant distress and temporarily impair overall functioning.

Another triggering event or memory, in real life or in "flashbacks," occurs. The self-injurer once again reacts by becoming numb/dissociated or by becoming emotionally escalated, agitated, and anxious. The craving to self-injure comes on like a fast-moving train. The craving is not for the experience of marring up one's body, but for the experience of feeling relief by getting high or by getting calmed down and comfortably numb. Hence, the "to cut or not to cut" dilemma. If the self-injurer has hit bottom, or an ultimate low, with her self-injury addiction, she may want to stop. Now she is at a crossroads. When she reaches the decision point, she may give up and self-injure again—she can choose to relapse. Or, she can decide to try to refrain from self-injury no matter how hard it may be. She can search for more effective coping strategies instead.

The self-injurer who wants to recover must go through a relearning process. The goal is to become completely abstinent from self-injury and to learn to cope with life and all of its difficulties, experiences, and memories effectively. The anxiety/agitation and numbing/dissociative reactions to emotional triggers will diminish over time with continued abstinence. One must learn to ride it out and to tolerate the extreme psychological discomfort for a while.

This is similar to the relearning phase that alcoholics and addicts go through in the beginning of their recovery. The newly recovering self-injury addict often looks, acts, and feels like the newcomers who walk into the rooms of Alcoholics Anonymous and other Twelve Step meetings. It is hard to tell the difference, because there isn't much of one.

Diagnostic Research Criteria for Self-Injury DSM Inclusion

At the time of this writing, there is not yet a diagnostic category or listing for self-injury in the *Diagnostic and Statistical Manual of Mental Disorders* (published by the American Psychiatric Association). But there should be. The *DSM* is the book, the main reference guide, that psychiatrists, psychologists, and other mental health professionals use for making diagnoses. Self-injury is only briefly mentioned as one of the possible criteria in a long list under Diagnostic Criteria for 301.83 Borderline Personality Disorder: "(5) recurrent suicidal behavior, gestures, or threats, or self-mutilating behavior."

The self-injurious behavior syndrome is a disorder of its own. It most closely fits the *DSM* criteria for and should be included as a specific Impulse-Control Disorder: Not Elsewhere Classified. As self-injury becomes increasingly addictive, it has many of the same characteristics as in the *DSM* Substance-Related Disorders category, and a few that are more specific. The following is a set of criteria, according to *DSM* system, design, and wording, that warrants further research and development for inclusion in a future edition of this manual.

♦ Research Criteria for (#XXX.X) Self-Injurious Behavior Syndrome

A pervasive pattern of deliberate mutilation of one's own body with the intent to cause injury or damage, but without suicidal intent, in order to provide relief from an intolerable emotional state, usually beginning in adolescence, and marked by the following:

(1) recurrent impulses to physically harm oneself

(2) intrusive, obsessional thoughts about self-injuring

(3) intolerable, increasing states of emotional anxiety and agitation and/or emotional numbing and dissociation

(4) feelings of both physical and psychological relief after the act of self-injury

(5) multiple episodes of self-injury

(6) low lethality

(7) impulsivity in other areas that are potentially self-destructive (e.g., alcohol or substance abuse; eating disorders; high-risk or dangerous behaviors such as reckless driving or becoming involved in abusive interpersonal relationships)

(8) a general pervasive mood of depression or anxiety

The following proposed *Diagnostic and Statistical Manual of Mental Disorders* research criteria for Self-Injury Dependence and Problematic Excessive Self-Injury (akin to Substance Abuse) are derived from much of the same criteria used to describe Substance-Related Disorders. When the problem of self-injury becomes addictive, it fits into this same basic framework. There are remarkable similarities. Much of the same wording in the *DSM-IV* applies and is used here for descriptive purposes.

✦ Research Criteria for Self-Injury Dependence

A repetitive pattern of self-injury leading to clinically significant impairment or distress, as manifested by three or more of the following:

(1) tolerance, as defined by either of the following:
    (a) a need for markedly increased and more severe episodes of self-injury to achieve the desired effect
    (b) markedly diminished effect with continued self-injury at previous levels of intensity
(2) withdrawal, as manifested by either of the following:
    (a) increased symptoms of distress when first stopping the behavior
    (b) repeated episodes of self-injury or addiction substitution (e.g., use of a substance such as alcohol or drugs) taken to relieve or avoid withdrawal symptoms
(3) the self-injury is more severe, causes more physical damage, is more physically dangerous, or occurs over a longer time period than was *intended*
(4) there is a persistent desire or unsuccessful efforts to decrease or control the self-injury
(5) a great deal of time is spent recovering from the immediate effects of the self-injury incident (e.g., tending to serious wounds; physical exhaustion)

(6) important social, work, or recreational activities are given up or reduced *because* of the self-injury

(7) the self-injury is continued despite *knowledge* of having a persistent or recurrent physical or psychological problem that is likely to have been caused by or made worse by the self-injury (e.g., recurrent self-injury despite recognition of the resulting feelings of depression, worthlessness, and regret; continued self-injury despite recognition that the body is becoming significantly marked up or disfigured from cuts or burns)

Specify if:

With Physiological Dependence: evidence of tolerance or withdrawal (i.e., either Item 1 or 2, or both, are present)

Without Physiological Dependence: no evidence of tolerance or withdrawal (i.e., neither Item 1 or 2 is present)

✦ Research Criteria for Problematic Excessive Self-Injury (akin to Substance Abuse)

A. A repetitive pattern of self-injury leading to clinically significant impairment or distress, as manifested by the following:

(1) recurrent self-injury resulting in failure to fulfill major responsibilities at work, school, home, or in the community (e.g., repeated school absences and/or poor academic

performance; neglect of children or household chores)

(2) recurrent self-injury that becomes significantly dangerous

(3) continued self-injury despite having persistent or recurrent social problems, or problems in relating to other people, caused by or
made worse by the effects of self-injury (e.g.,
being avoided or seen as an "outcast" by
one's friends or peers; arguing with parents
or significant others about the consequences
of self-injury)

B. The symptoms have never met the criteria for
Self-Injury Dependence.

The next chapter looks at addiction substitution and explains how other addictions typically come into play in the
life of the struggling self-injurer. Alcohol, drugs, anorexia
and bulimia, and behavioral addictions such as sex and love
addiction are discussed.

CHAPTER THREE

The "Addictions Shuffle"
Other Chemical and Behavioral Addictions

The addict, including the self-injurer, may keep running from one temporary fix to another, be it alcohol, drugs, or some other self-destructive behavior. Addiction substitution is more common than not, particularly when the recovering alcoholic or addict begins to face the difficult emotions that were previously suppressed. The initial impulse is to run away, once again.

Often, people who are in early recovery start using another chemical or behavioral substitute, typically one which they perceive to be "not as bad." For example: "I only drink beer now, not hard liquor," or "I only smoke marijuana now; I don't do real drugs," or "I don't use razor blades anymore; that was too dangerous. Now I only use my fingernails or car keys." The goal of escaping or getting high is still the same. Shuffling from one addiction to another, along with the process of denial or trying to justify continuing destructive behavior, functions only to keep people locked in an addictive cycle.

Many self-injurers have problems with alcohol and/or drugs. Even if they are not using right now, it is likely that they have in the past and are definitely at risk in the future.

There is an even higher correlation between self-injury and eating disorders, which many describe as behavioral addictions. Eating disorders include anorexia, bulimia, and compulsive overeating/obesity.

Self-injurers and other addicts are also vulnerable to other unhealthy behavioral addictions. Some of the more common ones include compulsive exercise; sexual addictions (including compulsive Internet sexual behavior); compulsive shopping, debting, and spending; workaholism; and codependency and addictive relationships.

Alcohol, Drugs, and Self-Injury

Favazza and Conterio (1989), in their study of 240 female habitual self-mutilators, found that 28 percent reported that they are concerned about their drinking; 18 percent consider themselves alcoholics; and 30 percent have used street drugs (mainly marijuana, "speed," cocaine, and "downers"). Forty-one percent of respondents reported that their self-mutilative behavior occurs while under the influence of alcohol or drugs: sometimes (26 percent), often (12 percent), and always (3 percent). Seventy-one percent consider their self-mutilative behavior to be an addiction.

Researchers Zlotnick et al. (1997) assessed 85 substance-abusing and substance-dependent inpatients who had histories of distressing traumatic events versus those who did not. Traumatic events included natural and man-made disaster; physical or sexual assault; rape; witnessing family physical violence; serious accident; robbed/mugged/physically attacked. The patients who had experienced traumatic events reported (1) more self-mutilative acts, (2) higher levels of dissociation, and (3) a greater degree of impulsivity than did patients without such histories. Impulsive behavior was defined as "any act that disregarded the action's long-term negative effects" and include behaviors such as binge eating, shoplifting, sexual disinhibition, and gambling. (By this definition, impulsive behavior can also include substance abuse/dependence and self-mutilative acts. However, for the purposes of their research, the authors used these categories for comparative purposes.)

In a study of data collected from hospital records of children and adolescent self-mutilators (age five to nineteen years old) in a psychiatric hospital setting, Simpson and Porter (1981) found that "many subjects compulsively ate, abused alcohol and drugs, and sliced, burned, or pulled hair from their bodies." Most of these children and adolescents had a history of physical and/or sexual abuse by family members. The authors state in conclusion, "It is suggested that self-mutilation may be a plausible and effective, if somewhat sensational, defense that is designed to handle stress by reducing painful emotional trauma."

Friedman (1989) found in his study of adolescents in the United Kingdom that those who had come from an unhealthy or inadequate environment *and* were lacking in self-esteem were more likely to develop behaviors that were dangerous to their health. These include "precocious and unprotected sexual behavior; the use of tobacco, alcohol, and other drugs; injuries arising accidentally from risk-taking behaviors, especially when combined with alcohol or drugs; intentional injury whether self-inflicted or inflicted by others; and poor eating and habits of hygiene." The responsibility for making positive choices, for health-enhancing behaviors, ultimately lies with the adolescents.

Thus, we see that self-injury very often happens concurrently with alcohol and/or substance abuse, as well as along with other maladaptive, and especially impulsive, behaviors. Self-injury while "under the influence" is extremely dangerous, like drunk driving. The self-injurer may get more than she bargained for, getting into an "accident" with her self-injury, which although unintentional, can result in her death. Like a drunken race-car driver, she could easily crash and burn.

The authors Zlotnick et al. state that it is important for those treating patients with substance abuse to know whether dissociation, impulsivity, and self-mutilative behavior are a reaction to trauma or a result of substance abuse. Research about cause and effect is surprisingly lacking. All of these areas should be appropriately addressed in treatment. For instance, the alcoholic self-injurer absolutely must address both her alcoholism and her self-injury addiction. Although one of these may presently be more life threatening, the other can soon take its place. When she is ready to deal with her emotions from the trauma of the past, she needs to move forward with this. However, she must at all times keep her addictions in check, maintain abstinence, and be aware of the potential for *addiction substitution*.

Sandra, a brilliant girl in her early twenties who dropped out of her Ivy League law school on the East Coast because she could not keep up, was found by the police lying down on a park bench in the snow. She was rushed to the hospital, this time with cardiac arrhythmia brought on by her bulimic episodes. With medical monitoring and intensive outpatient therapy, which addressed her depression, mania, borderline personality disorder (with some episodes of self-mutilation), and numerous issues with trauma and sexuality due to having been sexually abused as a child and then raped as a young adult, Sandra improved significantly. Her bulimia was well under control—but she was soon brought into the hospital emergency room again, after being found by the police on a park bench, this time passed out from an overdose of prescription drugs and alcohol. Her consulting psychiatrist, who was initially not aware of the severity of her alcohol and drug problems, made the referral to Alcoholics Anonymous. Sandra began attending AA meetings on a daily basis and continued with her intensive outpatient therapy for trauma as well as with medical follow-up as required. All of this contributed greatly to her recovery.

Eating Disorders and Self-Injury

Self-injurers are at high risk for eating disorders (anorexia nervosa, bulimia nervosa, and obesity/compulsive overeating), and vice versa. According to the *Diagnostic and Statistical Manual of Mental Disorders* (*DSM-IV* edition, American Psychiatric Association 1994), eating disorders are characterized by severe disturbances in eating behavior. There are two specific diagnoses: anorexia nervosa and bulimia nervosa. The majority of anorexics and bulimics are female, and most symptoms start during adolescence.

Anorexia nervosa is characterized by a refusal to maintain a normal body weight (less than 85 percent of that which is expected for one's height and weight) or a refusal to make expected weight gain during a period of growth (especially during puberty), which results in a weight that is less than 85 percent of that which is expected. Although underweight, the anorexic has a distorted sense of body image and sees herself as "fat." The anorexic has an intense fear of gaining weight and typically is in denial of the seriousness of her deteriorating physical condition, no matter what other people say (including doctors). Menstrual periods are absent (amenorrhea) due to the effects of her physical disease.

There are two types of anorexia: *binge-eating/purging type,* in which one regularly goes on eating binges (eating massive amounts of food) and then either throws up or uses laxatives, diuretics, or enemas to get rid of the food; and *restricting type,* in which one does *not* regularly engage in binge-eating or purging behaviors. Many anorexics also engage in compulsive strenuous physical exercise, sometimes to the point of injury or exhaustion, as an attempt to promote weight loss.

Bulimia nervosa is when one engages in repeated episodes of binge-eating, followed by inappropriate behaviors to try to get rid of the food and thus prevent unwanted weight gain. Such inappropriate behaviors to compensate may include throwing up, using laxatives, diuretics, or enemas; or fasting; or excessive exercise. There is a sense of "going out of control" with eating during an episode, usually followed by extreme feelings of depression, guilt, and worthlessness. To meet the *DSM-IV* diagnostic criteria, the food binges and compensating behaviors must both occur on the average of at least twice a week for three months.

However, as a clinician, I have known of teens and young adult women who would force themselves to vomit several times in one day, as many as three to eight times, every day. Debbie, an attractive, friendly sixteen-year-old girl of average weight with a nice figure, was one of them. She did not consider herself pretty, although everyone else did. She "looked good," so much so that when admitted to a hospital inpatient eating disorders unit for adolescents, a nurse commented, "What's she doing here? She seems like a normal, healthy teenager!" Although Debbie appeared to excel rapidly in the hospital's treatment program, as she did with school, sports, and other activities, no real progress in recovery had been made.

Until . . . one day a hospital counselor found Debbie collapsed on the bathroom floor after dinner, in a state of medical emergency. Somehow, Debbie managed to continue to hide her numerous bulimic episodes, which she finally admitted to staff had been occurring two or three times a day (usually after meals), even while in the hospital. On being found by the counselor, she commented: "I didn't lock the door 'cause I wanted someone to find me. It's better if somebody comes in, like you did."

Debbie eventually completed the hospital treatment program and returned home to her parents, who both faithfully participated in family therapy during her hospital stay. She continued treatment for her eating disorder in outpatient therapy in her hometown, with the continued dedication and support of her family.

For the bulimic, feelings of self-worth are unduly influenced by body shape and weight. Bulimics are typically not underweight, and they do not meet the criteria for anorexia—their weight is usually at, or somewhat above, average.

The *purging type* bulimic regularly engages in self-induced vomiting or the misuse of laxatives, diuretics, or enemas. The *nonpurging type* bulimic does not do these things, but instead uses other inappropriate behaviors to prevent weight gain, such as fasting or excessive exercise.

Obesity or *compulsive overeating* are not in the *DSM-IV* because it has not been established that these are consistently associated with a psychological or behavioral syndrome. However, simple obesity is included in the *International Classification of Diseases (ICD)* as a general medical condition. Obesity and compulsive overeating have been discussed extensively in the clinical literature in terms of having psychological factors, especially regarding what the causes are.

A common point of view is that some people use food and overeating as a way to escape from their difficult or uncomfortable emotions. The focus is on food instead, which can become an obsession, or even an addiction, that overshadows one's thoughts and feelings. There are Twelve Step groups such as Overeaters Anonymous (OA) for compulsive overeaters to deal with their food problems, like Alcoholics Anonymous is for alcoholics to deal with alcohol problems. Many times anorexics and bulimics also attend Overeaters Anonymous meetings, because their "drug of choice" also happens to be food. There are even OA meetings with specific focus on anorexia and bulimia, as these are considered the "flip side" of the same disorder.

The psychological and medical literature over the years frequently mentions the coexistence of self-mutilation and eating disorders. The literature mostly focuses on anorexia and self-injury and bulimia and self-injury.

In the 1989 study of 240 female habitual self-mutilators (ages fourteen to seventy-one), researchers Favazza and Conterio found that eating disorders were reported by 61 percent of the subjects surveyed.

In a 2000 study of 236 patients from an outpatient eating disorders unit, consisting of patients with restricting anorexia and binge-eating/purging anorexia and bulimia, researchers Favaro and Santonastaso found a very high frequency of self-injurious behaviors. These behaviors included skin cutting/burning; suicide attempts; substance/alcohol abuse; hair pulling; and severe nail biting. "Any" of the aforementioned forms of self-injury was reported by 59 to 76 percent of the patients. Skin cutting/burning was reported by 13 to 27 percent of patients; hair pulling by 31 to 44 percent of patients; and severe nail biting by 31 to 50 percent of patients.

Reasons Why: Eating Disorders

A person can become caught in an addictive cycle with anorexia, bulimia, or compulsive overeating/obesity for a number of different reasons. Developing an obsession with

food and with one's physical body in order to suppress difficult emotions is primary.

Teenagers and young women who already have low self-
esteem and perfectionist strivings are especially vulnerable
to buying into what is supposed to be beautiful and fashion-
able, according to what is portrayed in the media and in society. Models in fashion magazines as well as movie stars
are often too thin for their own good, to the point of being
physically unhealthy. There is a major focus in society on
losing weight and being thin, especially in terms of the rampant advertising for weight-loss centers, health spas and exercise clubs, faddish diets, and low-calorie diet foods. One
study showed that 60 to 70 percent of American women are
on some sort of a diet at any given time.

Control issues are another big reason, especially in
anorexia. Sometimes a bright, accommodating teenager,
for example, feels trapped by other people's expectations
and thus seeks to define her individuality and independence. She therefore seizes control of the one thing she can
that is uniquely hers—her own physical body. The more
people criticize her about her eating habits and express
concern and distress over her deteriorating physical condition, the greater her sense of autonomy and achievement.
It's a feeling of power.

As a clinician, I have also seen very young children go on
"hunger strikes," refusing to eat or being extremely finicky
about what they will and won't eat, oftentimes sending
their parents into a frantic tailspin. In each of three cases
that come to mind (all girls, ages five, six, and eight), the
children were extremely angry and felt that they had no
control over, or were entrapped by, some horrible event or
situation that occurred in their young lives. (Janie, the five-
year-old, was temporarily taken away from her mother and
put into the foster care system when her mother made a

suicide attempt and was placed in a mental institution. Julie, a six-year-old from Taiwan, had already endured several surgeries in her young life and was on an extended trip to America with her grandmother and aunt to see a world-famous neurosurgeon. Ling, the eight-year-old, had come over to America from Cambodia with relatives after her father had been shot. At the time of his death, she was holding his hand.) Two of the girls were also selectively mute (they could talk, but refused to talk to anyone—even family members). One thing that each of these children had in common was a shy but mischievous smile (as if to say, "Good, it worked!") when their mothers, teachers at school, and other concerned adults became frantic and at their wit's end when trying to get their child to eat.

One alternative explanation for anorexia is that the anorexic feels threatened by the process of physical maturation. The biological and physical changes, including menstruation and the surfacing of sexual feelings, are frightening. She strives to avoid it. By merciless dieting, the anorexic ensures a preadolescent figure. She prefers to remain childlike, or even utterly unappealing, to potential romantic suitors. Oftentimes, anorexic and compulsive overeater/obese women who were physically or sexually abused in childhood attempt to take control of the appearance of their physical bodies, trying to make them unattractive as a protection against further abuse.

There are similar biophysiological processes that connect anorexia, bulimia, self-injury, and other addictions. Although it is not the effect that is initially sought after, at least on a conscious level, anorexics, bulimics, and self-injurers eventually come to discover remarkable fringe benefits to their self-destructive behavior as their condition worsens to the point of becoming an addiction. These might include getting high and emotional escape. Bulimics often describe a "high" that comes on with repetitive vomiting, as do self-injurers with repetitive episodes of cutting and burning. This is due to a release of endorphins, as well as feeling a sense of profound psychological relief. Anorexics, and particularly those who engage in compulsive exercise, often describe feelings of high energy, increased physical and mental well-being, and feeling high. "The manic pursuit of exercise and creating a lean, taut body, so commonly seen among restrictor anorexic patients, purveys a sense of freedom, of invincibility, of physical lightness—almost like flying" (Cross 1993).

In a writing exercise that all clinical and medical staff members were required to do and share with each other during initial staff training before coming to work on an adolescent eating disorders unit (most of us had recovered from some sort of eating disorder), I described my battle with and successful recovery from anorexia nervosa as a teenager. I was twenty-eight years old, in graduate school, and working at the time.

I wrote: "I did go on eating binges, but not very often. My main thing was starving—i.e., having 'competitions' with myself to see how long I could go without food, which would last sometimes for several days. What I did seem to strive for with the starvation trip was going into different (non-chemically induced) mind states. After not eating for long periods of time, strange things happened, like getting an extreme 'high' or 'rush.' A lot of this was brought on in conjunction with extremely strenuous non-stop exercise. But the feeling I liked best was 'blanking out,' just going away and feeling nothing. I lived for it."

Self-injury brought on the exact same feelings and occurred very often between the ages of eleven and fifteen when I was struggling with anorexia. Self-injury seemed to intensify the feelings of high and escape brought on by the eating disorder, and vice versa. For me, the self-injury was ultimately much harder to give up, probably because I got away with it for so long. It was easy enough to hide the scars on my arms by wearing long sleeves all the time.

What's the Connection?

A number of similarities exist between eating disorders and self-injury. First of all, both disorders most frequently occur in females (although they do occur in males, who typically have more severe cases), beginning during adolescence. Both eating disorders and delicate self-mutilation symptoms have an "emotionally cathartic, self-purifying function in that they modulate states of anxiety, sexual tension, anger or dissociated emptiness, and they bring about a tremendous quasi-physical sense of relief" (Cross 1993).

Both those with eating disorders, particularly anorexia, and those who self-injure have intense control issues— wanting and attempting to be in control of their own bodies, minds, rights as a person, and life in general. Many have "perfectionist" strivings. One severely anorexic teenage patient who was an A student in school, captain of her cheer-leading team, and exceptionally beautiful stated, "I'm not really that good in anything, so at least I can be good at anorexia."

Those with eating disorders (including anorexia, bulimia, and obesity/compulsive overeating) and those who self-injure often have a history of abuse in childhood. Most often it is child sexual abuse, including incest. This is especially true when both an eating disorder and self-injury are present, which may occur simultaneously or at different times. Those with eating disorders and those who self-injure tend to come from dysfunctional, if not horrendous, family backgrounds. Anorexics and self-injurers tend to have alcoholic fathers and mothers who are absent or at least emotionally distant, have emotional problems, or have a high number of psychosomatic complaints. Bulimics often have mothers who are unhealthily overweight or obese. Self-injurers and those with eating disorders, especially anorexia and bulimia, have a high occurrence of alcohol and/or drug addiction, as well as other behavioral addictions, and problems with interpersonal relationships.

Issues with sexuality are typically present and oftentimes seriously problematic. This usually results from having been abused as a child, particularly if one was sexually abused by a trusted adult. The subsequent fear of being controlled or "attacked" by another person, albeit on a subconscious level, takes over. The feelings that are especially hard for self-injurers and those with anorexia to tolerate are

1. dependency
2. anger
3. sexual arousal
4. mixed messages from other people, which cause confusion and frustration

When these feelings occur at the same time or in reference to a particular situation or person (for example, in an unhealthy romantic relationship), the combination is overwhelming. The ultimate goal for the struggling anorexic or self-injurer is that these feelings must somehow be kept underground. In eating disorders, especially in anorexia, there is a suppression of sexual feelings because the body is too busy doing something else.

At the very least, sexuality is confusing or unduly stressful.

Anorexics and obese/compulsive overeaters tend to avoid sexually intimate relationships, either by making their bodies appear prepubescent and unattractive or by creating a large protective barrier of body fat between themselves and other people. Self-injurers disfigure their bodies and prefer to spend a lot of time alone, in isolation from other people. Romantic relationships are sometimes avoided because of the fear of scars, wounds, and hidden self-injurious behaviors being discovered. Many bulimics tend to act out sexually and often exhibit sexually promiscuous behaviors, have multiple partners with no emotional connection, have a high level of impulsivity, and use poor judgment. Generally speaking, bulimics are having (a lot of) sex. Anorexics are not having sex.

In particular, those who indulge in self-injurious behavior and purging behavior together can't recognize and identify emotions or sensations of hunger and safety. Self-injury in eating-disordered patients not only serves as an alternative tension releasing method to binge eating, but allows them to experience their bodies and seek a sense of reality and identity. In general, more serious psychiatric problems may be found in patients with eating disorders who purge than in those who only restrict their food intake without purging. In anorexics who engage in purging behaviors, both suicide attempts and self-injurious behavior are much more common than with those who practice food-restricting behaviors only. Those who employ more than one purging behavior, in both anorexia and bulimia, report a greater frequency of self-injurious behavior. Specifically, impulsive self-injurious behaviors such as skin cutting and burning are more frequent.

Self-injurious behavior is reported to occur at higher rates for bulimics than for anorexics. Compulsive self-injurious behaviors such as hair pulling are habitual, repetitive, and characterized by greater resistance to treatment. Among bulimics, compulsive self-injurious behavior is strongly associated with low awareness of one's internal emotional states and dynamics, and high obsessionality.

Because of the coexistence of and high associations among these disorders, the researchers/authors Favazza, DeRosear, and Conterio (1989) have proposed that the *DSM-IV* should list self-mutilation as an associated feature or complication of anorexia nervosa/bulimia nervosa. It is further stated in their article that the combination of self-mutilation, anorexia, bulimia, and other symptoms may be manifestations of an impulse control disorder known as the deliberate self-harm syndrome.

Addiction Similarities: Anorexia, Bulimia, and Self-Injury

Self-injury and abnormal eating habits both have the potential to become addictive. As so proficiently stated by clinical and research psychologist Dr. Lisa Cross in her article "Body and Self in Feminine Development: Implications for Eating Disorders and Delicate Self-Mutilation" (1993):

> The preoccupation with the physical self takes a more ego-alien form when the self-cutting or abnormal eating habits become addictive. These acts, which originally were aimed at erasing the existence of the body and at establishing self-control, now take control themselves. The world narrows to an obsessive preoccupation with the body and its products and the next meal, the next purge, the next self-cutting. Every plan for the day revolves around finding an opportunity to carry out these rituals.

Dr. Cross further states in her conclusion:

> The body, of course, comes to resent its taskmaster, in a way quite similar to the development of an addiction. The more the addicts attempt to control their emotional

world with drugs or alcohol, the more substance-dependent and out of control they become. Similarly, the body of the eating disorder or self-cutting patient escapes control and inflicts its own persecution: Vomiting leads to remorseless hunger; overuse of laxatives leads to intransigent constipation and laxative addiction; weight loss leads to an escalating compulsion to lose even more weight; self-cutting is never as fully satisfying an emotional catharsis and leads to a strong temptation to cut more frequently and more injuriously.

Hence, an addict of any type is an addict. Some types of addictions and "drugs of choice" (or "behaviors of choice") are more closely related than others. There are remarkably similar dynamics between anorexia and bulimia and self-injury. An addict is more likely to shift to something most closely related to her primary addiction. What particular drug or behavior this will be depends on what core internal dynamics are present and on what effect is being sought.

Behavioral Addictions

There are numerous behavioral addictions that are prevalent in today's society. New behavioral addictions (and literature and Twelve Step groups to address them) are springing up all the time. Today, there are Internet addictions, including Internet dating and cybersex. Even young children are becoming addicted to playing video games, which sometimes interferes with doing their homework and appropriately socializing with their peers. These things were not even around until a few years ago.

Many people are looking for some sort of relief from the stresses of everyday life or for something to fulfill an emptiness inside. It is easy for one to accidentally fall prey to one or more various obsessions and compulsions. It is when some type of obsessive or compulsive behavior becomes more important than, or interferes with, one's health, work or school, finances, interpersonal relationships, and/or responsibilities that it becomes problematic or addictive, and thus should be appropriately addressed.

Claudia got into an almost daily habit of stopping at the local mall on her way home from work. Although shopping was her favorite way to escape and relax after teaching special education high school students all day, her compulsive shopping and spending caused her to rack up a lot of credit card debt, which she could not pay. Claudia came to avoid the responsibility of paying her other bills on time, such as the rent, telephone, and electricity. She sometimes did not even open her mail and screened her phone calls to avoid creditors. Replacing something as uninteresting as the tires on her car, even when they became worn down to the point of jeopardizing her safety, was not a consideration of hers. She was constantly borrowing money from her mother, who was sometimes sympathetic and sometimes angry about it. This greatly added to the dysfunction in their already dysfunctional relationship. Claudia's behavioral addiction of shopping and spending thus interfered with her finances, other responsibilities, and an interpersonal relationship (with her mother). This only added significantly more stress in her life.

Too much of anything is not good. For instance, food is a good thing, it is necessary for survival, and exercise is good for one's physical health and psychological well-being. However, these and other things can easily become addictions if used excessively or inappropriately. The key is to have a healthy *balance* in one's life.

Some of the most common behavioral addictions among self-injurers, next to eating disorders, are exercise addiction, compulsive shopping and spending, and sex and love addiction.

Exercise Addiction

Exercise addiction occurs when the frequency, duration, and intensity of exercising becomes damaging to one's physical health and/or fits the criteria for addiction, in terms of interfering with other important areas of one's life. Exercise addiction is also closely correlated with anorexia and bulimia, and is quite common especially among food-restricting anorexics.

An exercise addict becomes preoccupied with the act of exercising, as well as with body image. Anorexics and bulimics are focused on losing weight and being thin; body builders and power lifters are focused on attaining muscle mass and physical strength. Those who are especially prone to exercise addiction include dancers, gymnasts, competitive athletes, wrestlers, and long-distance runners.

As with deliberate self-injury (for example, by cutting or burning), during strenuous physical exercise, the body's own natural endorphins are released in response to pain. Greater intensity, duration, and/or frequency of exercise may be needed over time to produce similar effects. The "runner's high," for instance, is experienced when the body pushes itself past its limits—however, taking it too far may lead to physical collapse or injury. Like other addicts, the exercise addict continues despite the consequences. Athletic performance may actually suffer. Physical withdrawal symptoms are rare but include changes in appetite, sleep, and increased sensitivity and decreased tolerance to pain. Psychological withdrawal symptoms may include depression, anxiety, or anger, hostility, and rage.

Additionally, exercise addicts are likely to also abuse

drugs. Anabolic steroids and growth hormones are sometimes used by weight lifters and body builders to produce rapid muscle and weight gain. Sometimes diuretics and anti-wasting HIV drugs are also inappropriately used. Other "performance enhancing" drugs and substances often abused by exercise addicts of all types include pain, muscle relaxant, and anti-inflammatory drugs; "speed"; beta blockers; and nutritional supplements and foods.

Compulsive Shopping and Spending

Compulsive shopping and spending is another addiction that a self-injurer may be likely to slip into, especially because this is most prevalent in females, especially teenagers and young women; women with eating disorders, especially bulimia; women who have a history of childhood sexual abuse; upper-middle-class teens and young women. All of these characteristics fit the profile of the typical self-injurer.

Compulsive shopping can easily become another highly *impulsive* behavior, which is fun, exciting, social, and a favorite pastime of many women. However, it typically leads to spending, frequently much more money than one actually has, and using poor judgment. Especially with the availability of credit cards, one can quickly get into significant financial debt or not have enough money to pay for the general necessities of life. Needless to say, this can cause significant stress and anxiety.

Teenagers and young adult women "shopaholics" who are into the fashion scene often buy a lot of clothes, sometimes that they do not even wear. Even on her moderate teacher's salary, Claudia, who was also a compulsive overeater, bought so many clothes on one shopping trip that she did not realize that she had bought two jeans jackets that were exactly the same. She ended up eating nickel-and-dime vending-machine junk food, such as chips and licorice, for lunch every day until her next paycheck and had to borrow a few dollars from a co-worker to buy Pepto-Bismol. (No, she did not take any of her new clothes back to the mall!)

There is a notably high rate of compulsive shopping among the subgroups of "beauty and fashion conscious" young women with anorexia and bulimia, particularly for those who have bulimia. For the struggling bulimic, shopping serves the purpose of filling the internal emptiness and provides something else to focus on, something else to obsess about, instead of facing what is going on with oneself emotionally. For the same reasons, there is also a correlation with child sexual abuse and compulsive shopping, and hoarding of possessions, in later years.

Sex and Love Addiction

Sexual addiction can be understood as a physical, emotional, and spiritual illness. In their book *Sex, Lies, and Forgiveness,* Schneider and Schneider define *sexual addiction* as "the pursuit of the sexual high to the exclusion of one's primary relationships, jobs, and health."

Sex, love, and romantic relationships are oftentimes difficult for self-injurers, those with eating disorders (especially anorexia and bulimia), and for those who were sexually abused as children. When two or more of these preexisting conditions are present, the probability is much higher that problem behaviors, or at least bad feelings, regarding sexuality will eventually surface. And those with concurrent alcohol and/or substance abuse problems are even more likely to use poor judgment, be prone to indiscriminate acting-out behavior, or be easily taken advantage of by others who use their vulnerability for selfish opportunity.

For some, sexual issues become a preoccupation, and

sexual behavior may become inappropriate, compulsive, and eventually another problematic addiction. An extreme need for dependency, made worse by low self-esteem, often leads one to run from one romantic relationship to another, or to desperately "look for love in all the wrong places," or to stay in negative, or possibly even abusive, romantic relationships that lead to utter destruction of one's sense of self. Additionally, "love" and "lust" are often confused. Someone inevitably ends up getting hurt.

Others may avoid sex and romantic relationships, for reasons such as fear of emotional closeness, rejection, being out of control, or further abuse at the hands of another person.

The Big Book of Alcoholics Anonymous (Alcoholics Anonymous) and other Twelve Step literature refer to problems with sex and relationships, and making amends to others who have been hurt by this behavior, as it is quite common among alcoholics. "If sex problems are bothersome, one must throw themselves all the more into helping others" (Twenty-Four Hours a Day, Hazelden 1975). Alcohol and drugs can cause people to lose their inhibitions when drinking or using. Drugs such as cocaine and stimulants can build a false sense of self-esteem and grandiosity. Designer drugs such as Ecstasy and nightclub drugs, intended for those who want to have a good time on the social scene, have often led young people to catastrophes such as date rape and death. The combination of alcohol or drugs and addictive sexual behavior is especially dangerous.

One of the main things that drive alcoholics and addicts to relapse is disappointment in romantic relationships—ask any therapist who works with alcoholics and addicts or any person who regularly attends AA or other Twelve Step meetings! Romantic relationships are an especially vulnerable area for self-injury addicts. Sex and love addiction will most likely, if not inevitably, lead to disappointment and heartbreak. In combination or substitution for any other addiction, it can cause one to go around and around in a vicious cycle.

Child Sexual Abuse, Cross-Addictions, and Relapse

In an academic journal article, "The Role of Incest Issues in Relapse" (Young 1990), it is stated that relapse is often related to uncovering painful early childhood incest experiences that have been defended against through self-destructive addictive behaviors. Comprehensive studies have established that relapse has been the most common outcome of recovery programs that treat addictive behaviors. However, the possible existence of childhood sexual abuse issues as a predisposing factor of relapse, and the connection between cross-addiction and relapse, needs to be more fully explored.

Young further states that another aspect of relapse is the phenomenon of multi-addictions: Withdrawal from an identified addictive behavior will often lead to the unmasking of other addictive behaviors. Relapse may indicate the existence of additional addictions that must be identified and explored in order for recovery to proceed. Additionally, sex and love addiction is often found in conjunction with alcoholism, codependency, and compulsive overeating, and often comes to light through the emergence of incest memories. Treatment of this hidden addiction (that is, sex and love addiction) is called for.

Self-injury is another possible "hidden addiction" that should be explored, and treated if present. This is because it is highly correlated with child sexual abuse and incest, as well as with the above-mentioned addictions.

Relapse Prevention

Relapse is the recurrence of addictive behavior after a period of abstinence. There are variable opinions among scientists, clinicians, and treatment approaches, including the Twelve Step approach, as to what exactly constitutes a relapse. For example, some define an alcohol relapse as "when one drinks X amount of alcohol over X period of time after X amount of time abstinent" and others define relapse as "any alcohol at all—even one sip." This is a source of great controversy in the addictions field.

Rigorous honesty with oneself is essential in recovery. Commitment is sacred. Abstinence means honest, complete, and total abstinence. It is too easy to play games, even in one's own mind, with words and definitions about how much is too much. And addiction substitution is another danger always lurking in the background. Why play with fire?

However, if one does relapse, it is helpful to see the relapse as a "slip" or a "temporary setback" and not a failure. Whatever gains (for example, in treatment; in therapy; in a Twelve Step program) that have been made have *not* all been lost. It is like hitting a speed bump or a pothole (although maybe a big pothole) on the great road of life. It is important to get back on track as soon as possible.

It is important for a recovering addict to be aware of her own *internal danger signals* that may lead to a potential relapse. The self-injurer may recognize, for example, "I'm angry! I'm emotionally escalated! I'm in a *huge* fight with my boyfriend! Romantic relationships are my danger area!" She can then wisely choose positive alternatives instead of having another self-injury episode. This may include removing herself from the negative situation, seeking support, and using some of her tools for relapse prevention. In Alcoholics Anonymous, there is a popular saying: "Never get too Hungry, Angry, Lonely, or Tired (HALT)." There are times when one needs to take positive action immediately, including seeking additional support.

Especially in early recovery, and at times when life becomes difficult for whatever reason, it is good for the recovering addict to have a game plan for *relapse prevention*. A therapist can be very helpful in devising such a plan that is specific to the individual's needs. Friends, significant others, Twelve Step program sponsors, and other concerned people in the addict's everyday life can help a recovering addict successfully carry out the relapse prevention plan.

CHAPTER FOUR

Childhood, Psychological, and Emotional Factors

People who suffer from self-injury are usually struggling with other psychological and emotional conditions as well. Sometimes, the resulting emotions from past history of childhood physical or sexual abuse, emotional abuse, or neglect, rape, or other trauma are just too overwhelming.

The relationship between commonly associated, psychologically based clinical and personality disorders are described and discussed in this chapter. Often, self-injurers are not diagnosed at all, incorrectly diagnosed, or correctly but incompletely diagnosed. For example, they may be clinically depressed, but there is more to the depression. Not all depressed people self-injure. And not all self-injurers are clinically depressed. At present, there is no diagnostic criteria for self-injury or established guidelines that are used by mental health professionals or medical doctors. There should be, and in chapter 2 of this book, this has been proposed.

The most common clinical and personality diagnoses among self-injurers are post-traumatic stress disorder; dissociative disorders; mood disorders (which cover depression and bipolar disorder, formerly known as manic-depression); anxiety disorders; impulse-control disorders; and borderline personality disorder.

Additionally, self-injurers often have problems with interpersonal relationships. These may include, for example, codependency; adult children of alcoholics issues; abusive romantic relationships, domestic violence, and the battered wife syndrome; and other problems with relating to other people (for example, due to fear, lack of trust, abandonment issues, inability to emotionally bond with others, and isolation).

Childhood Physical Abuse, Sexual Abuse, Neglect, and Trauma

The clinical and research literature suggest a number of conditions that might predispose an individual to self-injurious behavior. These include loss of a parent, childhood illness or surgery, childhood sexual or physical abuse, alcoholism in the family, witnessing family violence, peer conflict, intimacy problems, body alienation, and impulse-control disorders (Walsh and Rosen 1988). Recently, the association between trauma and self-destructive behavior has been enhanced by reports of self-mutilation starting after rape and after war trauma. Of these predisposing factors, recent research has focused on childhood sexual and physical abuse as being associated most powerfully with the development of self-injurious behaviors.

Green (1978) found that 41 percent of a group of physically and sexually abused children engaged in head banging, biting, burning, and cutting. This researcher concluded that the self-injurious behavior, which is often enhanced by the ego deficits and impaired impulse control of the abused children, seemed to represent a *learned pattern* originating from early painful traumatic experiences with hostile primary persons. Briere and Gil (1998) found that self-mutilation, examined in samples of the general population, clinical groups, and self-identified self-mutilators, was reported by 4 percent of the general and 21 percent of the clinical sample, and was equally prevalent among males and females. Childhood sexual abuse was associated with self-mutilation in both clinical and nonclinical samples. Results of this research suggest that the self-injury behavior is used to decrease dissociation, emotional distress, and posttraumatic symptoms.

A study by Lipschitz et al. (1999) found that childhood sexual abuse and emotional neglect were significantly associated with adolescent self-mutilation and suicidal ideation. The finding that emotional neglect was more strongly associated with suicidal ideation and self-mutilation than physical abuse was somewhat unexpected.

Clinical reports suggest that many adults who engage in self-destructive behavior have histories of trauma in childhood as well as disrupted parental care. Van der Kolk, Perry, and Herman (1991) conducted a study of young adults ages eighteen to thirty-nine to examine how histories of childhood trauma and disruptions in parental caregiving are related to suicide, self-injurious behavior, eating disorders, and dissociation. The study participants were gathered from clinical settings at Cambridge Hospital, from advertisements in local Boston area newspapers, and from the local probation department. Findings were that histories of childhood sexual and physical abuse were highly significant predictors of self-cutting and suicide attempts. On follow-up, the adults with the most severe histories of separation and neglect, and those with past sexual abuse, *continued* being self-destructive. The authors of this study conclude that "Childhood trauma contributes to the initiation of self-destructive behavior, but lack of secure attachments helps maintain it. Patients who repetitively attempt suicide or engage in chronic self-cutting are prone to react to current stresses as a return of childhood trauma, neglect, and abandonment. Experiences related to interpersonal safety, anger, and emotional needs may precipitate dissociative episodes and self-destructive behavior."

There is some controversy among researchers and clinicians in the mental health field as to the effects of childhood neglect. Some maintain that the effects of physical abuse and sexual abuse are far worse, as these result in bodily injury. Broken bones, lacerations, and burns are immediately visible and more readily accepted as evidence that something bad has occurred, and thus tend to be seen as more traumatic.

How can a "nonevent" such as childhood neglect be "traumatic"? The following case study will help you to understand.

Children at Risk: Reena and Jeremiah

Reena and Jeremiah were cute. Six-year-old Reena was referred for a psychoeducational evaluation at her elementary school, for possible attention deficit hyperactivity disorder and severe emotional disturbance. Her five-year-old brother, Jeremiah, had already been placed in a special day class for children with multiple psychological problems and learning disabilities by the time he was in kindergarten.

The brother and sister were taken in by a caring single foster mother, along with her own young children. This was already their third placement, after having been removed from the care of their own mother, who was currently in the women's state prison for prostitution and selling drugs. The mother was a known crack addict herself. There was some question by authorities as to whether one or both of the children were "drug babies." The kids had different fathers, who were nowhere to be found, and no other known relatives.

Court records indicated no reported physical or sexual abuse, but did indicate a severe case of neglect. Reena and Jeremiah were left alone in a cold, dark, roach- and rodent-infested basement room, with no heat in the winter, and nothing to eat, sometimes for days at a time, when their mother went "out." Feelings of extreme fear, terror, anxiety, and abandonment, and not knowing when—or if—Mom, or somebody, would come back to get them went on and on. And on . . .

Even two years later, with a lot of love and attention from the foster mother and her family, the school, the ever-involved (and ever-changing) social workers from the county court system, and some outside therapy at a community mental health center, both children looked permanently terrorized. Their eyes were always wide open, as if they had just seen a horror movie, but the picture never went away. Both children were always on the alert, were easily startled, said they had scary dreams (but they could not say about what), and were emotionally closed down. When asked about their mother or what happened, they did not say a word to anyone and looked as if they were far away.

Both children had behavior problems at school and at home. In addition to not paying attention in class, being disruptive, and not being able to focus on her schoolwork, the little girl was flirtatious and highly sexualized, like a young teenager. She sometimes bit her nails and would suck her thumb until it was red and raw. Both children, especially the boy, hit, kicked, bit, and punched their classmates and were intensely disliked by most of their peers. The boy broke a lot of things at school.

Like many other children who have been severely abused

and/or neglected, Reena and Jeremiah were much more "accident prone" than other children. They would tend to get a lot of playground-type scrapes and bruises from running, jumping, falling, and general clumsiness. Sometimes they did not even notice their own scraped knees and elbows and minor bleeding. Most kids would at least ask for a bandage.

One day the foster mother came in and told the school principal, "I had to call the county. They're taking the kids to another foster placement; I don't know where. The boy sleepwalks, and he starts fires. He almost burned my house down. I couldn't take it anymore, and I was afraid for the safety of my own family. Reena and Jeremiah won't be coming to this school anymore."

Children who have been so severely abused or neglected and traumatized, and at such a young age, are at very high risk for ongoing psychological problems. If the original trauma is not resolved and put to rest for good, addictions of various types, especially alcohol or drug addiction or self-injury, are most likely to surface in teenage years. It is hoped that the many children out there like Reena and Jeremiah will receive the best therapeutic interventions possible, and as early as possible, to prevent further damage. A stable, warm, loving, and safe home, one that is a permanent security base with consistent parental caregiving, is also needed.

Associated Clinical and Personality Disorders

People with a serious problem of self-injury who come to the attention of mental health clinicians are usually given a clinical diagnosis when they get into treatment. This helps clinicians to categorize the symptoms, for example, of depression or anxiety, and to be able to make better decisions for treatment planning and recommendations according to what has helped other people with similar symptoms in the past. This is also useful for medical doctors and psychiatrists to make decisions regarding the possible use of prescription medications. Additionally, most medical insurance companies require a diagnosis to bill for treatment.

Self-injury is seen among three categories of psychological disorders: (1) organic mental disorders, (2) psychotic disorders, and (3) neurotic disorders. While the type of self-injury we discuss in this book is strictly of the "neurotic disorder" category, a short definition of the other two categories of psychological disorders will be given here.

In terms of organic mental disorders, self-mutilation is a widespread problem among some people with severe mental retardation. It is also seen in other developmental disorders beginning in early childhood such as Lesch-Nyhan syndrome, and in certain neurological conditions such as Tourette's syndrome in which mental retardation does not occur. Self-mutilation has also been described in association with temporal lobe dysfunction. The cause of the behavior is organic and the self-injury is of an impulsive, repetitive nature without deliberate intent to hurt oneself.

Psychotic people differ in that they injure themselves in response to profound disorders of thought or perception. They do not realize the irrationality of their actions. The self-injury is not of a stereotyped, repetitive variety, but rather one or more discrete acts, which are usually bizarre or drastic in their form and have some sort of symbolic meaning. Sometimes the psychotic person maintains that he was under the control of an "outside force" (for example, hearing voices) or that he was acting in accordance with a biblical command (for example, castration or gouging out his eye because it caused him to sin). The self-injury may be a response to command hallucinations or delusions, particularly with religious themes.

People with neurotic disorders who have the problem of self-injury are seen as "normal" functioning people with depressive, anxious, or obsessive-compulsive symptoms. Here we are talking about, for example, the teenage self-injurer in high school who has an irresistible impulse to cut herself and experiences an intolerable building up of tension if this behavior is not continued. These individuals are well aware of the irrationality of the injury caused by the behavior and often try very hard to stop. As early as 1951, Zaidens theorized that "early fears and unexpressed rage toward a punitive and prohibitive parent lead to guilt and self-punishment in the form of neurotic self-mutilation."

The self-injurer may be given any of a number of clinical diagnoses, including those that address concurrent problems such as anorexia, bulimia, and substance-related disorders for alcohol and/or drugs. Because self-injurers frequently have a relevant history of child abuse, the *DSM-IV* "V-Code" diagnoses for physical abuse of child, sexual abuse of child, or neglect of child may be given. Child abuse and neglect are frequently a focus of clinical attention among children and teenagers who come to the attention of mental health professionals.

Both clinical and personality disorders are possible diagnoses for the self-injurer, either alone or concurrently. Clinical disorders involve anxiety, mood, and thought, whereas personality disorders involve characteristic dysfunctional personality traits and behaviors. According to the *DSM-IV,* in order to give the person a particular diagnosis, "the disturbance causes clinically significant distress or impairment in social, occupational, or other important areas of functioning."

I. Clinical Disorders Common in Self-Injurers

Post-Traumatic Stress Disorder

Post-traumatic stress disorder, commonly known as PTSD, is a syndrome defined by the intrusive reexperiencing of a trauma, avoidance of traumatic reminders, and persistent physiological arousal. PTSD is a diagnosis that describes symptoms experienced after the occurrence of an extreme traumatic event. Such traumatic events are defined as those that involve actual or threatened death or serious injury, or other threat to one's physical integrity.

The diagnosis of PTSD was first used to describe the severe and often disabling symptoms seen in Vietnam War veterans. The diagnostic label has been expanded over the years to include numerous other traumatic events besides war. Most frequently cited in the literature are childhood physical and sexual abuse, rape, and physical attacks such as robbing, mugging, torture, and kidnapping. The traumatic event may be experienced directly or witnessed or learned about in regard to another person. For example, one may witness severe domestic violence toward a parent or the death of a person in a car accident.

Because many self-injurers were physically and/or sexually abused as children or raped as adults and often have the characteristic symptoms of post-traumatic stress disorder, they are frequently given this diagnosis. Characteristic symptoms of PTSD include recurrent and intrusive recollections (memories) of the event that cause distress; recurrent dreams and nightmares; dissociative flashbacks; emotional numbing; feelings of detachment from others; and sense of a foreshortened future. This may lead to feelings of depression and hopelessness, and an overall impairment in one's ability to function. In PTSD, there are also persistent symptoms of increased arousal, such as hypervigilance, exaggerated startle response, difficulty sleeping, and diffi-culty concentrating.

As mentioned in the *DSM-IV,* post-traumatic stress dis-order may be especially severe or long lasting when the stressor is of human design (for example, torture or rape). Research has shown that one's understanding of what the trauma is matters. If someone intentionally hurts you, it adds a huge amount to the trauma. As the intensity of and physical proximity to the stressor increases, the likelihood of developing the disorder increases. Thus, children who were "trapped" in the homes of their abusers (for example, the abusive parent), over a period of time, and especially if the abuse was severe and occurred or began at a young age, are at especially high risk of developing PTSD.

Dissociation is a process associated with trauma in which the person is able to emotionally "numb out" and feel noth-ing. He or she feels as if the mind leaves the body and the immediate situation. This has been described by some people as "floating above the body," "not being there," and "spacing out." The mind is able to do internal cognitive tricks to escape. Dissociation is a rather sophisticated, higher-order defense mechanism. This subconscious process hap-pens seemingly automatically and can become a learned experience. However, states of emotional numbing and dis-sociation often become extremely uncomfortable, if not in-tolerable, and may lead to impairment in functioning. For example, it is hard to concentrate on the task at hand, be it walking down the street, learning in the classroom, or hav-ing a conversation with another person if one is feeling spaced out and not really there. Such states can be very dif-ficult to snap out of. Other avoidant strategies (that is, to avoid facing the traumatic event) may also be developed, such as self-injury and alcohol and drug use. For trauma victims, the good news about dissociation, self-injury, and drinking and using drugs is that it keeps one going. The bad news is that unless these avoidant strategies are given up, one never recovers.

Connors (1996) proposes in the clinical article "Self-Injury in Trauma Survivors: Functions and Meanings" that self-injury serves a number of functions that help childhood trauma survivors cope with posttraumatic events. First, self-injury is a reenactment of the original trauma, which can serve as an attempt to manage a previously unmanageable situation. ("This time, I'm in control of what happens; I'll be in charge of the pain and decide when it's too much.") It may also feel like the only way to retrieve nonverbal memories of past abuse, or to communicate to oneself and others about what happened. Second, the self-injury can serve as a vehicle for the expression of feelings and needs. Uncomfortable or forbidden feelings such as rage, frustration, guilt, shame, sexual arousal, sadness, and emotional longing are commonly released during a self-injuring episode. Another purpose of the self-injury is to express the depth of emotional pain that one is in (to oneself and/or to others) and to communicate one's needs for comfort and containment. A third purpose of the self-injury is to reorganize the self, to regain physiological and emotional balance. Connors states that many trauma survivors describe the calm that follows an act of self-injury. For example, cutting or gouging the skin may feel soothing, and tension is released or significantly reduced. The trauma survivor therefore regains a sense of homeostasis (balance). Fourth, self-injury is a way of managing the dissociative process. For some survivors of trauma, self-injury may serve as a "toggle switch" for the dissociative process: It may prevent one from dissociating or switching to an altered state (that is, the pain serves as an anchor to the present and allows one to avoid "going away"), or it may facilitate a switch into an altered state of

FIGURE 6. TRAUMATIC EVENTS THAT LEAD TO POST-TRAUMATIC STRESS DISORDER

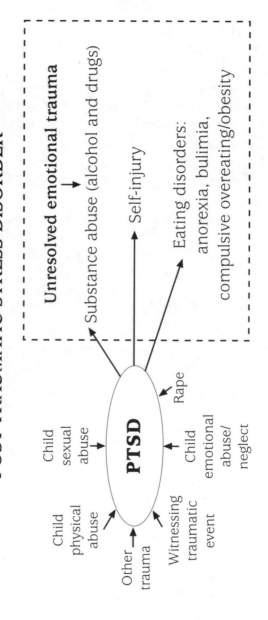

mind (for example, when one desires to disconnect from current distress). Some self-injurers describe both experiences.

Connors concludes: "Self-injury is an adaptive coping mechanism that makes a great deal of sense from the interior experience of the (childhood trauma) survivor. It is a method born of necessity and a child's perspective of the world. Early acts of self-injury may be reinforced by their effectiveness and become habitual, or manifested as compulsive behavior interlaced with substance or sexual addictions. This repetition may add another layer to the complexity surrounding the survivor's efforts to resist or change the behavior."

As illustrated in figure 6 on page 98, traumatic events such as child sexual abuse, child physical abuse, or rape may lead to post-traumatic stress disorder. If the emotional trauma remains unresolved, it may in turn lead to addictive disorders, such as alcohol or drug abuse, eating disorders, or self-injury.

Post-traumatic stress disorder and high-risk factors for addiction are listed in the following table.

PTSD and High-Risk Factors for Addiction

1. Isolation/lack of social support
2. Trauma occurred at young age (infancy/early childhood)
3. Long duration of or multiple episodes of traumatic event (for example, repeated childhood sexual abuse)
4. Pattern of repeated victimization (for example, abused as child; mean and abusive boyfriends as teenager; battered wife as adult)
5. Not able or not willing to talk about (to "vent" and verbalize) and *process* the traumatic experience

---

6. Unresolved/suppressed emotional issues resulting from the trauma (for example, anxiety, fear, terror)
7. Dissociative symptoms
8. Adolescent
9. Female (especially at risk for eating disorders and self-injury)
10. Confinement (for example, living in residential/ group home/ psychiatric/prison setting, or inner-city or war zone)

Anxiety Disorders

Post-traumatic stress disorder, as described above, is categorized as one of the *anxiety disorders*. Of all the anxiety disorders, this particular diagnosis has many specific features consistent with the background experiences and reactions of self-injurers. Other anxiety disorders especially prevalent in self-injurers include generalized anxiety disorder, panic attack, and obsessive-compulsive disorder.

According to *DSM-IV* criteria, the essential feature of *generalized anxiety disorder* is excessive anxiety and worry (apprehensive expectation, for example, waiting for something bad to happen; feelings of impending doom). Symptoms may include restlessness, feeling "on edge," irritability, difficulty sleeping, and difficulty concentrating or mind going blank. Some people with anxiety also have somatic complaints; that is, a lot of headaches, stomachaches, and other aches and pains. There may or may not be an actual medical basis for these complaints (for example, sometimes the doctor does not find any reason for the stomachaches, like an ulcer).

Children and teenagers with anxiety may be excessively

worried about their performance, may be perfectionistic, and may do the same task over and over to try to get it right. They may be constantly seeking approval and reassurance, especially from adults, that everything is okay. They may have difficulty concentrating on their schoolwork. They may be constantly worried about unlikely catastrophic events, such as earthquakes, tornadoes, or war, or their house burning down, or their parents suddenly dying in a car crash every time they go out.

Panic attack, according to the *DSM-IV,* is an extreme anxious reaction with sudden onset that involves intense fear and feelings of doom and an urgent desire to "escape." This involves emotional escalation, and is usually over in about ten minutes. Many times self-injurers receive this clinical diagnosis because panic attacks resemble the "escalation/ de-escalation" phase, as described in text and graphics in chapter 2. Other symptoms experienced during a panic attack may include racing heart, difficulty breathing (hyperventilating), sweating and shaking, and feelings of unreality or being detached from oneself.

According to *DSM-IV* criteria, *obsessive-compulsive disorder* involves recurrent thoughts, impulses, or images, along with repetitive behaviors (for example, compulsive hand-washing or counting) to attempt to alleviate the anxiety and distress. The thoughts and behaviors are intrusive and inappropriate, and take up a lot of time and energy from one's day. The obsessions or the compulsions may interfere with other activities and obligations, such as office work for adults or learning in the classroom for children and teenagers.

For self-injurers, the "to cut or not to cut, to cut or not to cut, to cut or not to cut" phase, as described in chapter 2, is an example of an obsession. The repetitive behavior of actual cutting or burning, time and time again, is an example of a compulsion. Many times self-injurers are given the diagnosis of obsessive-compulsive disorder (OCD) by mental health professionals because of these features.

A research study by Simeon et al. (1992) found that self-mutilators had significantly more anxiety than those who do not self-mutilate, as measured by the Schedule for Interviewing Borderlines and the Hamilton Depression Scale. Chronic somatic anxiety was significantly associated with the *degree* of self-mutilation. These researchers state, "Mounting anxiety has been clinically described as an important predictor in the escalating phase of self-mutilation. Mounting anxiety may be either a direct precipitant of self-mutilation, or the final common pathway to a variety of thoughts, affects, and experiences that trigger self-mutilating behavior." Relief of anxiety has been found in as many as 86 percent of self-mutilators in other research studies (Gardner and Gardner 1975).

Impulse-Control Disorders

Self-injurers are often described as highly impulsive in general. The self-mutilating behavior can at times be described as an impulsive reaction to stress, especially when one is extremely anxious, agitated, or angry.

The *DSM-IV* states that the main feature of *impulse-control disorders* is the "failure to resist an impulse, drive, or temptation to perform an act that is harmful to the person or to others." With most disorders of impulse control, the person feels an increasing sense of tension before committing the act. Afterward, one experiences a sense of gratification or "relief."

Impulse-control disorders described in the *DSM-IV* include but are not limited to kleptomania (stealing) and pyromania (fire setting). One of these impulse-control disorders, trichotillomania (the recurrent pulling out of one's own hair for the relief of tension, which produces noticeable hair loss) has at times been described in the clinical and research literature as a specific type of self-mutilating behavior.

However, there is no diagnosis specifically for self-injury. Self-injurers are sometimes given the *DSM-IV* diagnosis of "Impulse-Control Disorder NOS" (not otherwise specified). Researchers Simeon et al. (1992) propose that "self-mutilation might be best viewed as a distinct (DSM) Axis I impulse control disorder."

Dissociative Disorders

According to *DSM-IV* criteria, the essential feature of *dissociative disorders* is "a disruption in the usually integrated functions of consciousness, memory, identity, or perception of the environment." Feelings of dissociation and depersonalization are often described by self-injurers. Dissociation, depersonalization, and emotional numbing are especially prevalent in people who are also suffering with PTSD. There is a wide range of dissociative disorders, mostly depending on the severity and on the specific symptoms.

At the lower end of the spectrum is *depersonalization disorder,* characterized by a persistent or recurrent feeling of being "detached" from one's mental processes or body. At the higher (more severe) end of the spectrum is *dissociative identity disorder* (DID), which was formerly known as *multiple personality disorder* (MPD). However, this is an extremely controversial diagnosis; many clinical and medical professionals do not believe that this disorder exists. Furthermore, people who exhibit the clinical symptoms described in the diagnostic manual and in other literature (for example, that a person has two or more separate, distinct personalities, like in the infamous 1970s novel and movie *Sybil*) are extremely rare. Unfortunately, many people, including victims of severe child abuse and self-injurers, have been incorrectly diagnosed with multiple personality disorder or dissociative identity disorder.

Mood Disorders

Mood disorders include but are not limited to depression and bipolar disorder. What is now called bipolar disorder used to be known as manic-depression. According to the *DSM-IV*, the predominant feature across all mood disorders is a disturbance in mood. There are a range of clinical diagnostic terms under the category of mood disorders, depending on the particular symptoms and the frequency and severity of the symptoms.

Major depressive disorder is a severe form of depression. *Dysthymic disorder* is a less severe type of depression and is often (but not exclusively) used in diagnosing children and adolescents. Depressive symptoms may include feelings of sadness; worthlessness; hopelessness; lack of interest or pleasure in all or almost all activities, even those that one usually enjoys; thoughts of death or suicide; and problems with (that is, too much or too little) eating or sleeping. Some people who are depressed may have difficulty concentrating or fatigue or loss of energy. In children and adolescents, the depression may present itself as an irritable, agitated mood.

Bipolar disorder involves both depression and one or more manic episodes. People who have bipolar disorder are often described by others as extremely "moody" or as having mood swings. Manic episodes are a distinct period(s) of time in which the person's mood is notably elevated or irritable, and there is an increase in physical goal-directed activity. The person in a manic phase may present with nonstop talking, flighty ideas, racing thoughts, and a decreased need for sleep.

Research findings about self-injury and depression have been mixed. Most of the literature supports that depression is one of the most common underlying symptoms and clinical diagnoses among self-injurers. Researchers Dulit et al. (1994) found that *frequent* self-mutilators were significantly more likely to receive diagnoses of current major depression.

The researchers Simeon et al. (1992) found that self-injurers did *not* suffer from more depression than control (non-self-injuring) subjects on the Beck Depression Inventory. They also did not suffer from greater hopelessness. These researchers speculated that "the significant negative correlation between the degree of self-mutilation and hopelessness lends to the conceptualization as an act of self-healing through the transient restoration of more hopeful affect."

Many times the self-injurer does not look or act "depressed." She may not know it herself that depression is there, deep down, because she is masking these difficult feelings by her acting-out (self-injuring) behavior. As a matter of fact, she can often fly high above any painful emotion because of her self-inflicted physical pain. That is her goal.

Therefore, the self-injurer often goes unnoticed or at least the depth of her difficulties go unnoticed for a long, long time. Sometimes, not until the cutting/burning becomes a full-blown addictive disorder.

On standardized tests that measure depression and other symptoms (for example, the Beck Depression Inventory, the Hamilton Depression Scale, the Children's Depression Inventory, the Deveraux Behavior Scales, the Burkes' Behavior Scales) scores may even come up as "normal" (that is, not significantly depressed), according to the self-injurer's own perceptions as well as the perceptions of others in her life such as parents and teachers.

"It's the Quiet Kids I Worry About"
Experienced teachers and other school personnel will often say that it's the kids who are too quiet, are well behaved, and seem to get "lost in the shuffle" that they worry about the most. That is because they seem to be doing so well— despite having been through horrible trauma such as child sexual abuse. However, these are often the ones who are suffering the most, and the ones who need the most help.

Sophia, a quiet, rather nondescript ten-year-old girl, was in a special day class for children with learning disabilities. She did not show up with significant scores on the social-emotional part of her psychoeducational testing, but further observation and diagnosis over time revealed that she was in fact clinically depressed. Sophia had been repeatedly sexually abused by a teenage boy in her neighborhood when she was very young. Not able to concentrate on her schoolwork, she was having difficulties with reading and learning in general, but otherwise appeared as the role-model student in a class full of behaviorally acting-out, aggressive children (mostly boys) who were always getting into trouble. Except for occasionally appearing to "zone out" in the classroom when she was supposed to be doing her work, according to her seasoned, well-aware teacher, "She looked too good for what she had been through." Sophia was in a lot of emotional pain, quietly suffering in silence, occasionally lightly scratching her arm with a paper clip or a pencil . . .

Because of early counseling and intervention (that is, counseling by the school counselor; intensive therapy at a community mental health center; becoming involved in self-esteem-building activities that she liked and did well in, such as the school chorus) Sophia fared well. She was very soon also able to mainstream into the general education classroom because her reading and academic learning improved significantly.

II. Common Personality Disorders in Self-Injurers

Borderline personality disorder is one of the most common diagnoses given to self-injurers, as is post-traumatic stress disorder. Many times, there is also a concurrent clinical disorder, such as PTSD, an anxiety disorder, or a mood disorder (for example, major depression), which typically demands more immediate therapeutic intervention. Borderline personality disorder is certainly the most common one in self-injurers among the *DSM-IV* Axis II Personality Disorders and the only personality disorder with a significant amount of clinical and research literature regarding the connection to self-injury.

Borderline Personality Disorder

Borderline personality disorder is a complex personality disorder marked by mood swings, high-drama behaviors, emotional (especially angry) outbursts, serious problems with close interpersonal relationships, and an intense fear of abandonment. Other symptoms include a high degree of impulsivity (for example, reckless driving, sex, spending, substance abuse) and an instable self-image (for example, internal conflicts about sexual orientation, long-term goals, values). Behaviors toward others frequently include boundary violations, giving mixed messages, approach-avoidance conflicts, manipulation, anger provocation, and at first idealizing and then turning against another person. The title of a popular psychology book on this subject, *I Hate You, Don't Leave Me* (Kriesman and Straus 1991) is a good example of something that a borderline patient would be likely to say to someone (whether it is her significant other or her therapist) that effectively summarizes her painful internal chaos.

One of the possible nine indicators of borderline personality disorder, according to the *DSM-IV,* is "recurrent suicidal behavior, gestures, or threats, or self-mutilating behavior." The self-injurer must have at least five or more other symptoms or traits in order to make the diagnosis, which should be done with careful thought and caution. Although there is a very significant correlation, not all self-injurers have borderline personality disorder. And not all borderline patients have a problem with self-injury. Some may, or may not, have self-injured one or a couple of times as a form of manipulation and attention-seeking.

As previously mentioned, clinical literature and research results have shown a strong association between self-injury and a history of childhood abuse. Research results also demonstrate a strong association between diagnosis of borderline personality disorder and a history of childhood abuse. Herman, Perry, and van der Kolk (1989) found that significantly more (81 percent) borderline subjects than non-borderline subjects gave histories of childhood trauma, including physical abuse (71 percent), sexual abuse (68 percent), and witnessing serious domestic violence (62 percent).

A number of studies have shown an association between self-injury and reported histories of childhood sexual abuse in patients with borderline personality disorder. One study by van der Kolk, Perry, and Herman (1991) systematically explored how both childhood abuse and neglect relate to the development of self-destructive behavior. These researchers, using both historical and prospective data for people with personality disorders or bipolar II disorder, found that histories of childhood trauma, particularly sexual abuse, and histories of childhood neglect were highly significant predictors of chronic suicide attempts, cutting, and other self-injurious behavior. In this study, the borderline diagnosis was the only diagnosis significantly associated with physically self-destructive behavior.

Problems with Relationships

Most older adolescent and adult self-injurers will tell you that they have had a "difficult childhood," to say the least. Many were severely abused, sometimes by their own parent, stepparent, or other family member, or were not safe and protected by and within their own families. Many were neglected or emotionally and verbally ripped to shreds by adults in their lives who were supposed to nurture and care. Many had parents who were alcoholics or drug addicts. Many had a parent or parents who were in one way or another not there.

It is thus difficult for the struggling self-injurer, especially while in the throes of her addiction, to trust other people or to develop healthy, close interpersonal relationships with others. Self-injurers tend to spend a lot of time alone, sometimes to indulge in the cutting/burning behavior, and sometimes just because isolation seems preferable to being around other people and the possibility of getting hurt, again. As with other types of addicts, her primary relationship will be with the addictive substance or behavior of choice, and with herself.

The self-injurer coming from such a traumatic childhood background may inadvertently seem to choose negative people as friends or romantic partners. For example, she may have an alcoholic boyfriend or a husband who batters her. Something may seem to draw the self-injury addict in to the unhealthy, the destructive, in others . . . maybe because it feels familiar, it reminds her of home; and deep down, she does not feel that she deserves anything better and that life will always be this bad.

It is quite common for problems of domestic violence, alcoholism, drug addiction, child abuse, and psychological problems to go on from generation to generation, and around and around in a vicious cycle, if not addressed, understood, and effectively dealt with.

Therapy can help the self-injurer to develop understanding, to change her negative and self-destructive ways of thinking, and to help build self-esteem and self-confidence. The recovering self-injurer may also attend Twelve Step groups that are relevant to her, such as Adult Children of Alcoholics, Al-Anon, or Codependents Anonymous, to address relationship issues. In these groups, she can learn how to have a healthy, functional relationship first with herself and then with other people.

CHAPTER FIVE

Why Now?

History and Increasing Incidence of Self-Injury

The self-mutilation syndrome has received increasing attention both theoretically and descriptively in psychiatric literature during recent years (Simpson and Porter 1981). There
has also been an increase in the general public's awareness
of this problem since 1997, when Princess Diana's admission of being a self-injurer on national television brought
widespread attention to the problem. Even with recent
media, books, and other publications, there is still a lot to be
done in terms of increasing the general public's awareness
as well as *understanding* of the problem of self-injury. Because of all the recent media attention to the problem of self-
injury, many self-injurers and their families (for example,
parents in hopes of helping their teenage daughters who are
struggling with this problem) are likely to seek treatment.

Most important, there is a great need to "demystify" the
disorder and to offer practical treatment options, as has been
done with anorexia nervosa and bulimia over the course of
the last twenty or thirty years. It is important that we (professionals, parents, and the general public) no longer cringe
in fear, go into a panic, or freeze in astonished amazement
when hearing about or seeing a teenage girl (or anyone else,

for that matter) who cuts or burns herself repeatedly, silently screaming for help.

Historical Overview of Self-Injury: Many Biblical/Religious Cases

Self-injury has been around for a long, long time. In the fifth century B.C., in book 6 of *History,* Herodotus describes a Spartan leader who deliberately and severely mutilated himself with a knife. Deliberate self-injury is also mentioned in the Bible: the Gospel of Mark 5:5 describes a man who "night and day would cry aloud among the tombs and cut himself with stones."

Self-mutilation resulting from religious delusions or extreme religious beliefs have occurred since before the time of Christ. They continue to occur to this day, although less frequently and only in those with severe psychosis, schizophrenia, and delusional intoxication. Documented cases of such acts demonstrate religious self-mutilation to either atone for sins (including sins of thought and sins of action) or for the purpose of appeasing one's God or gods.

A review of the existing literature on self-mutilation accompanying religious delusions shows that castration and enucleation (deliberate removal of one or both eyes) are the most common forms. Other acts include cutting off or otherwise injuring one's hand(s), slashing or burning one's flesh, and amputation of one's tongue.

Referring to biblical texts to explain acts of religious self-mutilation occurs among a number of (extreme pathological) self-mutilators. Probably the most commonly quoted passage is Matthew 5:29,30, which states, "And if thy right eye offend thee, pluck it out. And if thy right hand offend thee, cut it off." Consequently, some extreme religious self-mutilators are inclined to remove any body part that they feel causes them to commit, or even to think of, sin. Other verses in the Bible give examples of self-mutilation. In Matthew 19:12, eunuchs castrate themselves "for the sake of the Kingdom of Heaven." I Kings 18 describes a rain-making ceremony in which the priests of Baal gashed themselves with knives and lances until blood gushed.

Sometimes, such examples from the Bible and religious stories and examples are misinterpreted. They may be interpreted literally by some extremists to mean that self-mutilation or the amputation of a particular body part is necessary to demonstrate one's faith and to free oneself from sin. One may think that, for example, after all, how could such actions be wrong if they're portrayed in the Bible as being appropriate or even honorable in certain circumstances?

Clark (1981) in his article on self-mutilation and accompanying religious delusions makes recommendations for treatment and study of such extreme cases. These are attention to previous history or evidence of self-injury; attention to preoccupation with biblical passages regarding self-injury; attention to preceding drug abuse; and attention to early loss of the father in males. Rapid tranquilization and intensive psychotherapy are advised following hospitalization.

The "Holy Anorexics"

During medieval times, a number of women in search of piety, wishing to imitate the sufferings of Christ, would deliberately starve themselves and deliberately injure themselves by such methods as self-flagellation (that is, self-punishment by whipping), scourging and disfiguring their faces, and impaling their breasts with nails. Living lives of extreme deprivation, suffering, and charitable acts toward others was encouraged and applauded by priests. Many young girls idolized and wanted to be like these holy women, and imitated them, much like young teenage girls today imitate and dress like certain female pop stars.

One of the most famous and fully documented cases of the "Holy Anorexics" (women who starved themselves to death in pursuit of sanctity) was that of Saint Catherine of Sienna, who lived in the 1300s (Bell 1985). Her biography was a best-seller for two hundred years. When Catherine of Sienna was sixteen, her beloved older sister died, and her parents pressured her to marry her rich, older, disgusting brother-in-law. She panicked and embraced a life of radical piety and chastity. She cut off her long blonde hair, put an iron chain around her waist to ensure her virginity, wore a crude woolen shift, and limited her diet to bread, water, raw vegetables, and bitter herbs. She slept on a wooden board and indulged in self-punishment by whipping herself three times a day with the chain until she drew blood. The lack of food reduced her weight by half within months. She spent most of her time at her parents' home praying alone in a tiny cell underneath a flight of stairs, where she had visions and hallucinations (Egan 1999). No one could stop her from her chosen life of self-deprivation and self-punishment. She undertook a life of extensive charity, helping the sick and the dying. She was credited with having performed numerous miracles, such as multiplying loaves of bread to feed the poor. She attempted to organize a group of women to fast and pray for the success of the pope. When her efforts at renewing the papacy and the Church failed, she became despondent, even gave up water, and died three months later in 1380 at the age of thirty-three. She was canonized as a saint in 1460 (Bell 1985).

Other famous holy women of medieval times who endured such self-inflicted suffering and starvation include Saint Teresa of Avila, who went so far as to induce vomiting by poking the back of her throat with an olive twig before receiving Holy Communion (Callender 1999). Bridget of Sweden poured hot wax on her flesh, and Saint Clare of Assisi slept on the cold floor in the wintertime and fasted three days each week during Lent (Egan 1999). Saint Lucia was said to have avoided sexual temptation by cutting out her eyeballs.

Historical Overview of
Academic Literature on Self-Injury

Since the mid-nineteenth century, there have been numerous case-study-type articles in the medical literature about the more deviant forms of self-mutilation. These were primarily of severe psychotic individuals who engaged in isolated incidents of extreme self-mutilating behaviors (usually in response to religious delusions or hallucinations) such as the gouging out of eyeballs (enucleation) or castration. The first published article in the medical literature on self-injury, in 1846, was a case report of a forty-eight-year-old manic-depressive widow who took out both of her eyeballs. She did this because she felt that her eyes were causing her to desire men and therefore to "sin." Self-mutilation was for a long time considered a "symptom" of various mental disorders.

Other academic research and clinical literature up until the 1980s primarily covered medication trials and behavioral interventions used to treat profoundly retarded people, autistic people, and others with developmental disabilities. The focus was on individuals who engaged in the stereotypic, repetitive type of self-mutilation seen in organic disorders beginning in early childhood.

As early as 1934, Karl Menninger of the Menninger Clinic in Topeka, Kansas, wrote about self-mutilation from a psychoanalytic theoretical point of view. He believed that self-mutilation contained three essential elements: (1) aggression turned inward, often that which is felt toward an external love-hate object, usually a parent; (2) stimulation, with either a sexual or purely physical intent; and (3) a self-punishing function that allows the person to atone for an aggressive or sexual "sin." The great paradox is that while self-mutilation is self-punishing and self-destructive, it is also an attempt at self-healing.

Menninger (1934) wrote: "In any circumstance, however, while apparently a form of attenuated suicide, self-mutilation is actually a compromise formation to avert total annihilation, that is to say, suicide. In this sense it represents victory, sometimes a Pyrrhic victory, of the life instinct over the death instinct."

The trend in the academic literature from that time on, up until the late 1980s, was to vary from an extreme to a minimalizing point of view. Self-injury was sometimes seen as a form of "para-suicide" in which the person has suicidal ideation or intent. Sometimes the whole problem of self-injury was referred to as "wrist-cutting" or, according to Pao (1969), "delicate self-cutting," thus not considering the full scope of the problem.

In 1979, Morgan (in England) described a "delicate self-harm" syndrome. This included self-mutilation as well as drug overdoses and failed suicide attempts. In 1983, Pattison and Kahan reviewed fifty-six case reports of self-harm in the existing clinical literature and developed a model for the Deliberate Self-Harm Syndrome. According to this model, the syndrome involved

1. onset in late adolescence
2. multiple episodes of self-harm
3. multiple types of self-harm
4. low lethality

5. the behavior continues over many years
6. four predominant psychological symptoms (despair; anxiety; anger; cognitive constriction)
7. predisposing factors of lack of social support; homo-sexuality (in men); drug and alcohol abuse and suici-dal ideation (in women)
8. associated depression and psychosis

Drug overdoses and failed suicide attempts were ex-cluded from Pattison and Kahan's model of the Deliberate Self-Harm Syndrome. The syndrome was considered by these authors to be an impulse-control disorder.

In 1986, Lacey and Evans described the connection be-tween self-mutilation and other impulsive addictive disor-ders. Hence, they described the problem of self-injury and addiction substitution. They described a "multi-impulsive disorder" with interchangeable symptoms such as binge eating, substance abuse, kleptomania, and self-mutilation. These authors noted that people with this disorder tended to drift from clinic to clinic: "Thus, if alcohol abuse is ad-dressed in the alcohol treatment unit, the patient may stop drinking but moves to food or cutting."

It has long been known that addiction substitution hap-pens, unfortunately, more often than not. In order for an addict to *really* recover, a solemn and rigorously honest commitment to abstinence must be made. Underlying emotional issues as risk factors need to be addressed and dealt with, brought into awareness and understood.

In 1987, the groundbreaking work of Favazza high-lighted the idea that self-injury is distinct from suicide. His theoretical writing and empirical research did wonders in advancing our knowledge base and understanding of self-injury. Favazza states, "A basic understanding is that a per-son who truly attempts suicide seeks to end all feelings whereas a person who self-mutilates seeks to feel better." He also notes that it is important to be aware that repetitive self-cutters are at high risk for suicide, often by overdoses, secondary to demoralization over an inability to control their acts of self-harm (Favazza and Conterio 1989).

Categorizing Self-Injurious Behaviors

In his 1998 article, Favazza described a clinically useful classification of self-mutilation into three categories: major, stereotypic, and superficial/moderate. *Major* self-mutilation includes the infrequent, drastic acts such as eye removal (enucleation) and castration, which are associated with psychosis and intoxication. *Stereotypic* self-mutilation includes acts such as the head banging and self-biting often seen in individuals with Tourette's syndrome or severe mental retardation. *Superficial/moderate* self-mutilation includes compulsive acts such as skin picking and trichotillomania (the deliberate, repetitive act of pulling out one's own hair), as well as such episodic acts as skin cutting and burning, which evolve into a clinical syndrome of impulse dyscontrol with variable symptoms.

Furthermore, Favazza classified self-mutilation into three subtypes: compulsive, episodic, and repetitive. *Compulsive* self-mutilation involves a behavior that is automatic, without much thought put into it, that occurs in response to an irresistible urge and promotes relief. The most heavily researched type of compulsive self-mutilation is trichotillomania, repeatedly pulling out one's own hair. *Episodic* self-mutilating behaviors occur periodically (only every so often) as a symptom or as an associated feature in clinical disorders such as post-traumatic stress disorder, dissociative disorders, or borderline personality disorder.

Episodic self-mutilating behavior can turn into *repetitive* self-mutilation when the self-injuring behaviors become an overwhelming preoccupation. Repetitive self-mutilators may describe themselves as "addicted to" their self-injury. At this point, the self-injury seems to run its own course.

When a person presents with the problem of self-injury, for example, when there are visible self-inflicted cut marks, or when a verbal threat to harm oneself is made, mental health professionals need to quickly and accurately assess which one of three things may be going on (A, B, or C):

A. Is the purpose of the self-injury to commit suicide?
B. Is the purpose of the self-injury to try to manipulate somebody, or to get attention?
C. Is the purpose of the self-injury to relieve intolerable feelings (such as to alleviate anxiety/anger/emotional escalation or to escape emotional numbing/dissociation), and is the self-injury of the episodic or repetitive addictive type?

Then, the best decisions for what to do in the moment as well as long-term to help the person in need can be made. It is important to remember that sometimes a combination of two or more of these things may be going on. For example, a psychologist called me for consultation about how to help an adult woman patient with borderline personality disorder who threatened to drink cleaning fluids. She was attempting to get her therapist's attention, via a rather dramatic cry for help, and had a tendency to be histrionic, acting out, and inappropriately manipulative. When assessed at the hospital clinic, the woman was not suicidal and admitted to the attempt to get attention. However, further assessment over time revealed that the patient also had a problem with self-injury of type C. She was repeatedly indulging in various self-injurious behaviors when distressed and had one day come into her therapist's office having severely bit the inside of her mouth on both sides as well as her tongue, which was purple, swollen, and badly bruised.

Early and accurate assessment of the problem of self-injury and appropriate therapeutic intervention can help such women while the destructive behavior is merely episodic, before it becomes a full-blown addiction.

Prevalence of Self-Injury

Getting a true estimate of how often self-injury actually occurs in the general population is not possible. This is because it is a "hidden" disorder, like bulimia. It is easy to hide. Many self-injurers and the people in their lives do not even know that self-injury is a disorder, or have the words to explain it, or realize that other people have it too. Some would not admit to it, either to themselves or to anyone else, or do not think that it is a "problem" (like alcoholics or drug addicts who are in denial or who do not realize that their excessive drinking/using drugs has become a problem or an addiction).

Over the years, researchers have attempted to estimate how many people in the general population self-injure. At times the research methodology has been flawed, or biased, or both. One significant study by Briere and Gil (1998) used advertisements looking for people with a history of self-mutilation placed in popular magazines *(Good Housekeeping, Parents)* and publications for child abuse survivors *(Moving Forward, Treating Abuse Today),* and handouts that were distributed at abuse-survivor conferences on both the East and West Coasts. Not everyone reads those particular magazines, and not everyone is interested in or attends conferences. This study in particular excludes men, teenagers, and people of lower socioeconomic and educational backgrounds. Furthermore, the researchers were unable to tell which questionnaires that came back were from the magazine solicitations or the conference attendees. In another study reported in the same article, a national sampling service generated a stratified, random sampling of the United States, based on geographical locations of registered owners of automobiles and people with listed telephones. However, this tends to exclude teenagers (the largest proportion of self-injurers) and people who do not own cars or who do not have a telephone.

Briere and Gil's (1998) results from the aforementioned study were that self-mutilation was reported by 4 percent of the general and 21 percent of the clinical population, and it was equally prevalent in males and females. This prevalence is considerably greater than Walsh and Rosen's (1988) estimate of 14–600 cases per 100,000. Favazza (1998) writes that superficial/moderate self-mutilation (the most common form) occurs at a prevalence rate of at least 1,000 per 100,000 in the population per year. In a survey of 500 college students in America, 14 percent admitted to at least one episode of self-mutilation (Favazza, DeRosear, and Conterio 1989).

It has been somewhat easier (but still difficult) to get estimates of the prevalence of self-injurious behavior in clinical populations. Most of the studies include only those self-injurers who present for psychotherapy in clinics that serve abused children or trauma clinics, or for therapy in general, or who are in confined settings such as psychiatric hospitals, residential treatment centers, or prisons.

In reviewing the literature, Pattison and Kahan (1983) report that the vast majority of self-injury cases occur in late adolescence, particularly among violent and antisocial youth in institutional settings, with incidence rates as high as 40 percent.

In the landmark study of 240 female self-mutilators by

Favazza and Conterio (1989), child abuse was reported by 62 percent. Sixty-one percent admitted to having or having had an eating disorder in the past. There was also a significant association with alcohol and substance abuse.

As discussed in chapter 4, self-injury is strongly associated with certain clinical and personality disorders, such as post-traumatic stress disorder and borderline personality disorder. Some of the research studies over time have primarily focused on exploring the prevalence of self-injury in patients who have these specific disorders.

Is the problem of self-injury actually on the increase? There are a couple of factors that need to be considered when answering this question:

1. Self-injury has been around for a long time; it is only recently coming into the light regarding research, publications, media attention, and people who are seeking treatment, so now it is noticed and acknowledged more.

2. Self-injury is a learned behavior. There are some people who will "copy" the behaviors of others, however dysfunctional or destructive they may be. When I was living in a college dorm in the early 1980s, a group of girls on our floor were watching television in the lounge. There was a special on a late-night talk show about bulimia, which seemed to grab everyone's interest. Heidi, a severely overweight graduate student, loudly exclaimed, "I want to learn how to throw up, like that girl on TV, so I can lose weight. I'm serious, I want to become a bulimic!"

Contagious Self-Mutilation

The problem of self-mutilation as "contagious" or as an "epidemic" within treatment programs, hospitals, and especially with males in prisons has been described throughout the literature. The problem of contagion has generally been defined as "the infliction of self-injury by one individual and imitation by others in the immediate environment" (Rosen and Walsh 1989).

Episodes of contagious mutilation present a serious problem, because they generally create havoc in treatment settings or other environments in which they occur. Staff report feeling helpless and demoralized, and this behavior can certainly scare the living daylights out of other patients, residents, students, or anyone else who is in the immediate environment. Rosen and Walsh state, "Ultimately, self-mutilation contagion is likely to be best understood as an interaction of individual psychopathology with dysfunctional relationships in a given social context."

A group of consulting psychiatrists (Fenning, Carlson, and Fenning 1995) investigated an outbreak of contagious self-mutilation in a junior high school. Their observations were that the majority of adolescents involved in this behavior did *not* demonstrate any severe overt psychopathology. They had *not* been identified as "emotionally disturbed students." All of them belonged to the leading inner social circle in school. All of them excelled in their academic achievements. The behavior seemed to be contagious. Girls were more involved in the self-mutilating behavior than boys. *Isolating* the "hard core" students (those who initiated the self-mutilating behavior, with the more severe psychopathology, who "induced" the self-mutilating behavior in the more passive and less disturbed students) seemed to be the only effective means of controlling this contagious behavior.

Fenning, Carlson, and Fenning (1995) also state that self-mutilation may be more frequent in the educational systems than reported. Underreporting might be due to the reluctance to deal with this issue openly. These authors state that it is important (for psychiatric consultants) to

1. provide more information to educational systems
2. identify populations at high risk for self-mutilation
3. guide the (school) staff in their management of this highly contagious behavior

Males Who Self-Injure

The problem of self-injury is most often reported across the clinical and research literature in females, mainly in teenage girls and young adult women. Females tend to ask for help and to seek mental health treatment services such as psychotherapy more often than males do. Favazza (1992) writes, "The majority of repetitive self-mutilators who come to the attention of psychiatrists are females in their twenties, about two-thirds of whom report childhood sexual and/or physical abuse."

Many males in our society tend to avoid emotional expression that may involve getting in touch with difficult feelings, such as deep sadness, and at all costs may want to avoid crying. Some males may be concerned about not wanting to appear "weak" or "needy," so they may be reluctant to, or do not, seek help.

Self-injury does occur in males also, but much less frequently—just as with anorexia and bulimia. Male self-injurers tend to have more severe cases, for example, to cut or self-destruct more savagely, and to have more associated psychopathology, such as antisocial personality disorder. This may be at least in part because by the time male self-injurers come to the attention of treatment professionals, their self-injurious behaviors are well advanced and very serious.

Males tend to express their anger via physical aggression toward others, whereas females tend to turn their angry feelings inward, toward themselves.

The greatest concentration of males with the problem of self-injury are found in prisons. In prison settings, especially in heavy confinement, the self-mutilation problem can be spread "contagiously" and may reach epidemic proportions (Favazza 1992).

Over the years, there have been a number of studies about self-injurers in the prison system. Jones (1986) analyzed data collected from the case records of self-mutilating prisoners and compared this with a random sample of others in prison. Findings were that three-quarters of the self-injuring incidents took place in isolation cells or on prison psychiatric units. Injuries were the result of self-inflicted cuts. Statistical analyses revealed that the self-mutilators were more likely to already have scars on their wrists or forearms upon admission and were more likely to have attempted suicide while in prison. While they were incarcerated, the self-mutilators were also charged with more assaults, convicted of more felonies, and had more severe disciplinary actions taken against them.

In 1997, Fulwiler et al. conducted a study to explore how prisoners who injured themselves without intending to die would differ clinically from prisoners who had attempted suicide. Findings were that suicide attempt was associated with adult affective disorder, whereas self-mutilation was associated with a history of childhood hyperactivity and a mixed dysthymia/anxiety syndrome that began in childhood or early adolescence. Furthermore, the self-mutilators and those who attempted suicide had very different clinical presentations and histories.

Having worked as a consulting psychologist in a residential facility for teenage boys who are on court probation, I have seen numerous incidents of deliberate self-injury in males. A lot of the boys had scars on their forearms from cuts, and burns from cigarettes, cigarette lighters, and hot pennies. Most often, this would start off as a "dare" game, to see who was the strongest and the toughest. Sometimes it became compulsive.

Homemade tattoos have become increasingly popular over the years, with both teenage boys and girls, especially (but not only) with those who are gang affiliated. This behavior can also become compulsive and, needless to say, very dangerous in terms of getting (and spreading) infections, including HIV, from using dirty needles. At one time, two of the boys in the residential facility where I worked had even invented a homemade tattoo machine, using the cassette reels of a "boom box." It was quite an ingenious invention, albeit something negative and destructive. After the appropriate reprimands and consequences, staff encouraged these boys to put their brainpower into their schoolwork instead.

Characteristics Prevalent in Self-Injurers

Most of the literature describes characteristics of self-injury as seen in females, because they are the ones who most frequently come to treatment and who respond to surveys. Most prevalent background characteristics of self-injurers (which are discussed in detail throughout this book) are history of childhood abuse, including sexual abuse, physical abuse, and neglect; trauma, including post-traumatic stress disorder; current or past history of eating disorders; and current or past history of alcohol and/or substance abuse.

Other characteristics of self-injurers include an early history of surgical procedures or illness, accident-proneness, perfectionist tendencies, dissatisfaction with their body shape and sexual organs, and an inability to express feelings easily (Favazza 1992).

Conterio, Lader, and Bloom (1998), in their textbook *Bodily Harm,* point out certain prevalent themes as ones that recur among the self-injurers seen in the S.A.F.E. Alternatives inpatient treatment program:

1. difficulties in various areas of impulse control, as manifested in problems with eating behaviors or substance abuse
2. history of childhood illness; or severe illness or disability in a family member
3. low capacity to form and sustain stable relationships
4. fear of change
5. an inability or unwillingness to take adequate care of themselves
6. low self-esteem, coupled with a powerful need for love and acceptance from others
7. childhood histories of trauma or with significant parenting deficits. This leads to difficulties with internalizing positive nurturing
8. rigid, all or-nothing thinking (self-injurers often have catastrophic thinking such as "Nothing will ever change!") and/or perfectionism and workaholism

Profiles: What Does a Self-Injurer Look Like?

In their study of 240 female habitual self-mutilators, Favazza and Conterio (1989) describe a "typical" self-injurer:

> The typical subject is a 28-year-old Caucasian who first deliberately harmed herself at age 14. Skin cutting is her usual practice, but she has used other methods such as skin burning and self-hitting, and she has injured herself on at least 50 occasions. Her decision to self-mutilate is

impulsive and results in temporary relief from symptoms such as racing thoughts, depersonalization, and marked anxiety. She now has or has had an eating disorder, and may be concerned about her drinking. She has been a heavy utilizer of medical and mental health services, although treatment generally has been unsatisfactory. In desperation over her inability to control her self-mutilative behavior this typical subject has attempted suicide by a drug overdose.

I believe very strongly in early assessment and therapeutic intervention for children and adolescents, at the first sign of trouble, before problems escalate and take over a person's life, as happened to the twenty-eight-year-old self-injurer described above. For example, even a very young child who was physically or sexually abused can benefit greatly from some type of therapy, before resulting problems interfere with his or her school experience, learning, and life in general. The problem in assessing self-injury is that it is so easy to hide. Most teachers, parents, and professionals do not understand it, let alone know what to look for. In teenagers, a "typical" profile of a self-injurer may look something like this:

She is sixteen or seventeen years old; of any race or socioeconomic background; bright; attractive; does well academically; and on first impression, seems like a very "normal" teenager. She may be obsessing about her appearance and her weight, and you suspect that she may have, or may have had, problems with some type of an eating disorder such as anorexia or bulimia. She was most likely sexually or physically abused, or both, sometime in childhood. She comes from a family where there are other problems—for example, an alcoholic or drug-addicted parent; a parent or parents who are not there for her (e.g., they may be dead or in some way emotionally unavailable). She has probably experimented with alcohol and/or drugs more than the average teenager, sometimes overdoing it. She may already have an alcohol or drug problem. She seems emotionally closed down; a bit of a loner or aloof; often "moody"—sometimes quiet and depressed, and sometimes anxious, inappropriately angry, or agitated. She has a tendency to, in general, be highly impulsive. She sometimes looks as if she's "spacey" or in a world of her own. She may be sexually promiscuous, at least in the way she dresses, or she may avoid boys and dating altogether. She may be a bit of a perfectionist, have an air of uniqueness or independence about her, and she definitely has a mind of her own. She may complain of a lot of headaches or stomachaches, and starts missing a lot of time from school. Her grades may begin to drop, and she may start to slide academically—although she is bright, she can't seem to concentrate on her schoolwork. She begins to spend more and more time alone, in isolation. She always wears long sleeves, even in the summertime.

She may be your own daughter, or if you're a teenager, your best friend; or a student in your junior high or high school classroom who looks like she daydreams too much. She needs help.

Associated Feelings and Effects of Self-Injury

Favazza (1998) writes that "SM (Self-mutilation) can best be understood as a morbid self-help effort providing rapid but temporary relief from feelings of depersonalization, guilt, rejection, and boredom as well as hallucinations, sexual preoccupations, and chaotic thoughts." Favazza also states that self-mutilating behaviors provide temporary relief from the distressing symptoms of mounting anxiety, racing thoughts, and rapidly fluctuating emotions.

Among the effects of self-mutilating behavior are tension release; termination of depersonalization; euphoria; decreased troublesome or enhanced positive sexual feelings; release of anger; satisfaction from self-punishment; a sense of security, control, and uniqueness; manipulation of others; and relief from feelings of depression, loneliness, loss, and alienation (Favazza 1989).

Treatment: What Has Worked, Ideas for Intervention, and Future Directions

To date, most treatment approaches for self-injury have been based on theoretical notions as opposed to empirical studies that determine the efficacy of different treatment approaches. No one method or specific type of therapy seems to work better than any other for self-injury. Research on what works best and for whom, and the development of more effective therapeutic interventions, are called for.

We do know from the literature and clinical experience that behavioral therapy interventions have been used extensively and have shown some positive results in the treatment of stereotypic self-mutilation, especially for mentally retarded patients. In more severe cases, regarding all types of self-injury with its associated clinical symptoms such as depression and anxiety, the use of medication has sometimes been helpful.

Favazza (1998) points out that treatment is still problematic, especially for repetitive cutters and burners. He states that medication and new psychological approaches are helpful.

Briere and Gil (1998) state that treatment for self-injury may be most effective when it reduces painful affect and when it bolsters coping strategies. It may thus be helpful to treat self-mutilating clients not only by discouraging the self-mutilating behavior, but also by intervening in the conditions that keep it going. Briere and Gil suggest that effective interventions may include the following:

1. Most immediately, exploration of alternate methods of reducing distress that are less injurious or shame-inducing (for example, physical exercise, distraction via telephone or reading, changing environments [by going outdoors, moving to a different room, etc.] or contacting friends or hotlines when the desire for self-mutilating behavior is intense)
2. Teaching cognitive and behavioral strategies for dealing with stressful situations and painful internal states
3. Strengthening internal affect regulation capacities and strategies (ability to control internal emotional ups and downs), so that external methods like self-mutilating behavior become less necessary
4. Ultimately, reducing the distress and dissociative symptoms that may underlie and motivate involvement in self-mutilating behavior.
                            —(Briere 1996; Linehan 1993;
                                  Walsh and Rosen 1988)

Much work still needs to be done in terms of advancing the understanding of self-injury as well as in developing treatment strategies that work and in conducting research studies, as has been done for alcohol and drug addiction, and more recently for anorexia and bulimia over the last several years. Favazza (1998) points out that "the undeniable truth is that acts of self-mutilation are unnerving"—to most people, including medical and mental health professionals. He further states: "The impulsivity of repetitive cutters and burners is exasperating to deal with, but no more so than that of alcoholics."

PART TWO

A Plan for Recovery

CHAPTER SIX

Treatment Options

There are many treatment options that can be combined or used alone to help self-injurers stop hurting themselves and fully recover. This chapter will walk you through the various different types of psychological therapy and other treatment choices that are available and that can be useful. After reading this information, self-injuring clients (or, for example, a teenager's parents or caregivers) will know what to *expect* when they walk in the door.

Treatment options may include the following:

- individual therapy
- group therapy
- family and/or couples therapy
- psychopharmacological medication (antidepressants, etc.)
- inpatient hospital programs
- Twelve Step programs

Being open to trying (and combining) different treatment options, as appropriate to the self-injurer's specific needs, is more likely to bring a positive long-term outcome. The self-injurer may have different needs at different times. Different concerns predominate in the initial stages of recovery, after a period of prolonged abstinence (when one is capable of a dealing with the deeper emotional issues), and after many years in recovery when traumatic or stress-provoking "triggering" life events happen (such as the death of a loved one) that can make one prone to relapse.

. Because self-injury is most prevalent in teenagers, school psychologists, counselors, social workers, and school nurses (particularly those who work in junior high and high schools) are very likely to come across this sometimes "hidden" disorder in the course of their daily work and in their routine assessments, especially when assessing for serious emotional disturbance. Thus, a psychoeducational assessment is often the first step toward diagnosis and treatment recommendations.

However, psychological testing is not an essential first step to treatment. If a parent or caregiver, teacher, concerned other, or the self-injurer herself feel that there is a need for some sort of treatment or therapy, get help as soon as possible. For example, one can immediately make an appointment at a local community mental health center or with a private therapist.

What Is Psychological Testing?

Psychological testing can be of great benefit to anyone who is experiencing emotional, behavioral, cognitive, memory, or learning problems, especially if these problems are negatively affecting one's daily life. It is a quick and concise way to gather a lot of useful information to accurately target and evaluate areas of concern. One may be referred to a psychologist for an assessment by a school, mental health, or medical professional, or one may be self-referred.

The testing process primarily involves completing a series of paper-and-pencil tests and responding to verbal questions asked by an interviewer (the psychologist). There's nothing scary about it. Most people, including children and adolescents, enjoy the exclusive one-to-one attention and the opportunity to talk about themselves. Some of the tasks are fun, for example, those that involve drawing, puzzles, and building things with blocks. At worst, some of the tasks may become a bit tedious or "boring" for some people, such as having to do increasingly complex math problems or repeat long strings of words and numbers from memory.

Psychological testing is conducted for diagnostic purposes, educational and/or treatment planning, and for making recommendations. Psychological assessments may be educational, clinical, or neuropsychological in orientation. Sometimes these are combined.

Testing sessions are typically one to two hours long, sometimes a little longer, and involve a one-to-one interaction between the psychologist and the client. In cases with children, adolescents, and those who are gravely disabled, a parent or caretaker may be present for at least part of the session to give input.

Psychoeducational testing is a form of assessment that usually takes place in schools. For instance, a parent may be concerned that a child's emotional problems are affecting his or her learning, or a teacher notices that the child is bright but is not making academic progress, and thus suspects a learning disability. A referral is made to the school psychologist to conduct an assessment to figure out what is wrong, that is, the reasons why learning and academic progress are being affected—and what can be done about it.

Psychoeducational testing consists of first obtaining a complete educational history (review of report cards, teacher's comments and observations, etc.); conducting a health assessment, wherein a school nurse or a doctor gives a brief physical, visual, and auditory screening and reviews developmental and medical history; and obtaining information about family history and background.

Tests to evaluate cognitive capability, academic achievement, visual and motor processing, and social/emotional/personality dynamics are then given. There are numerous different tests in each of these categories that an evaluator may choose to use, according to what is most appropriate for the particular case referral reason. For instance, there are nonverbal tests for cognition that involve putting puzzle and pattern designs of increasing difficulty together that are culturally fair and sensitive to people for whom English is a second language. Academic tests measure skills in particular areas such as reading, mathematics, and written language that are compared to national norms regarding standard scores, percentile ranks, and age and grade levels. There are tests for visual processing where picture cards are shown and the person has to remember what was on them when taken away after ten seconds. There are behavior-rating checklists for teachers and parents to fill out. Projective (subjective) testing may involve drawing a picture or making up a story or verbally responding to incomplete sentences ("I like . . ."; "I feel sad when . . ."). The tests are scored, interpreted, and written up in a summary report.

Clinical psychological assessment is done to diagnose clinical and personality disorders, usually according to *DSM-IV* criteria, and for treatment planning. Medical/developmental history, family background, and usually a brief report on academic or career achievement are completed. Cognitive testing is next, usually some form of a traditional IQ test or alternative assessment. There are many well-established standardized paper-and-pencil tests for assessing depression, anxiety, and personality disorders (for example, the MMPI: Minnesota Multiphasic Personality Inventory and the

Beck Depression Inventory) as well as for other relevant factors such as drug and alcohol addiction severity, trauma, and career interests. Projective testing may include drawings, storytelling, or telling what you see in a series of ambiguous inkblots shown on picture cards (the Rorschach inkblot test). Additionally, some hospitals, treatment centers, and other agencies may include less formal, nonstandardized assessment instruments (for example, checklists and questionnaires) that have been developed internally. Tests are then scored and interpreted and written up in a summary report.

If cognitive impairment is suspected, such as caused by traumatic brain injury (for example, from a fall off a bicycle resulting in a concussion, a gunshot wound, or breathing noxious chemicals), a referral may be made to a neuropsychologist. He or she is a specialist in the field of psychology who has undergone extensive training in this particular area.

Neuropsychological assessment involves highly specialized psychological tests that are designated as indicators of organicity or brain damage. These tests of intellectual impairment target deficits in different mind functions. Chief among these functions are memory for newly learned material and perception of spatial relations. The tests are usually auditory memory and paper-and-pencil tests. The report generated is usually in addition to a clinical or psychoeducational report.

Clinical Psychotherapy: What to Expect

There are a number of different approaches and therapeutic techniques that clinical therapists use. Some therapists work primarily from a particular orientation, such as psychodynamic or cognitive-behavioral. Many therapists use an "eclectic" approach, combining different approaches and techniques that are most appropriate to the client and to the particular situation.

Individual therapy is between two people, the client and the therapist. Individual sessions may occur in different settings. These include private practice office settings, offices within institutions such as schools and hospitals, or within community mental health centers or hospital outpatient treatment centers. Therapy sessions are typically forty-five minutes to one hour. Many times clinicians use thirty-minute appointments for children and adolescents, because of their shorter attention span. *Couples* or *marriage therapy* involves the person's spouse or significant other. *Family therapy* may involve the client and one parent/guardian; both parents; stepparents; siblings (if they are old enough); and other important members of the extended family such as a grandparent who lives in the same house. *Group therapy* involves a therapist and possibly a co-therapist, and a small group of clients. Most groups have a specific purpose, such as grief and bereavement counseling, or groups for women survivors of sexual abuse. Some groups deal with more general issues relevant to a particular set of people, for example, patients in a recovery program or adolescents in a boys' or girls' group home for abused children.

Following is an overview of some of the most commonly used treatment approaches for addressing emotional issues and dysfunctional behaviors.

Emergency Treatment

Some self-injurers may need emergency intervention or hospitalization. One may need to be rushed to a hospital emergency room or community urgent care center because of a serious physical injury. A threat or an attempt to self-injure, just like a threat or an attempt to commit suicide, meets the first of the established criteria for psychiatric hospitalization, including involuntary commitment (if one is in danger of harming self; if one is in danger of harming others; if one is gravely disabled).

Suicide prevention telephone hotlines are a readily available resource. They may be called by one in danger or by a concerned other, such as a family member. In an acute crisis situation, a psychiatric emergency team (PET team) may be called to a person's home, school, or wherever she is for an assessment and intervention. The police can also become involved. A psychiatric unit may put the person in crisis mode on a seventy-two-hour hold to keep the person safe and for observation, which may be extended if needed.

While a self-injurer may require a longer stay at a hospital inpatient psychiatric unit, managed care and insurance companies may limit the time to less than what is optimal or necessary. That is why it is so important to follow up with outpatient therapy as soon as possible.

Crisis Intervention

Crisis intervention is a very brief (one to six sessions) form of therapy following a "crisis." Examples of a crisis include natural disasters such as an earthquake or a flood, or being physically assaulted, being raped, or getting mugged while walking down the street. By definition, the problem is a normal response to a stressful event. However, anxiety and tension predominate; the person is in shock and may be in denial, and her usual problem-solving strategies are not enough. The goal is to restore the person to her level of functioning before the crisis. This type of therapy is available immediately on demand—one does not have to wait for a scheduled appointment.

If one does not come to effectively cope with the crisis, she may be at high risk for depression, withdrawal, abusing alcohol or drugs, or other self-destructive behaviors. More extreme cases of unresolved crisis can result in post-traumatic stress disorder or major personality disorganization (confusion, inability to function, etc.).

Psychodynamic Psychotherapies

Psychodynamic therapies stem from the work of Sigmund Freud, who is known as "the father of psychology." His view was that dysfunctional behaviors are the result of unconscious conflicts that occurred during one's childhood. The goal of *psychoanalytic psychotherapy* is "to alleviate pathological symptoms by . . . (making) the unconscious conscious and . . . (reintegrating) previously repressed material into the total personality structure" (Shilling 1984).

Anxiety occurs when there is conflict between one's impulses, which are based on the need for immediate gratification, and what one should do according to rational, realistic means. What one feels that one should do according to internalized values and standards of society also plays into the conflict. When one is not able to resolve a conflict through rational, realistic means, she resorts to faulty defense mechanisms.

Defense mechanisms are unconscious and serve the purpose of denying or distorting reality. One defense mechanism, repression, serves the purpose of keeping disturbing thoughts and memories within the unconscious mind. For example, a self-injurer who was sexually abused as a child often represses memories of the original trauma. Another defense mechanism is fixation. This occurs when, as a result of an unresolved conflict or trauma during a particular stage of development, the person "gets stuck" in that stage.

Alcoholics and addicts, and self-injurers, in their attempts to keep what is too painful on an unconscious level, tend to remain fixated until they give up their addictive behaviors.

Psychoanalytic therapy involves treating emotional disorders by having the therapist work with the client to freely talk about herself, especially about early childhood experiences and about dreams. It is primarily a "talking therapy." The idea is that this emotional catharsis (venting), along with the therapist analyzing what is said, helps the client to develop insight. This in turn helps the client resolve internal conflicts. This process will reduce the internal anxiety that otherwise may lead to dysfunctional behaviors.

The primary goal of psychoanalysis is the analysis of personality. This is accomplished by exploring and figuring out the true meaning behind the client's free associations, transference, resistance, and dreams.

Free association requires the client to say whatever comes to mind, without censure or judgment—that is, without defenses. This process allows unconscious material to surface to the conscious. For example, Sigmund Freud believed that slips of the tongue are not mere accidents, but rather statements that provided meaningful information about what is hidden in the unconscious. Hence, the popular expression "Freudian slips."

A vital part of psychoanalysis involves exploring and working through the client's feelings of transference. *Transference* is the process in which the client typically projects onto the therapist feelings that she originally had for a parent or another significant person in the past (for example, an influential teacher or a grandparent). This occurs as the therapeutic relationship develops because the therapist is considered a neutral figure. The client's feelings can be either positive or negative, or both. Analyzing the transference helps the client to understand how she may not always accurately perceive, can misinterpret, and can respond to others in dysfunctional ways in the present because of past events.

For example, a female client who had an abusive father may project negative and hateful feelings toward an older male therapist. This is because she sees him as a father figure and is unconsciously afraid of him. The skilled therapist can use this experience to help the client understand her unconscious negative feelings and unrealistic fears pertaining to men in general that have previously played out in dysfunctional romantic relationships.

Resistance is when the client tries to run away from and avoid further exploration of unconscious material as it begins to surface, so as to avoid anxiety. For example, the client may start coming late for or missing appointments, remain silent, or bounce a check when paying the therapy bill. Resistance needs to be confronted and worked through in therapy. This helps the client learn how not to sabotage relationships with other people when she (unconsciously) feels that she is getting too close to them.

Dream analysis is used to uncover unconscious conflicts and motives. The client tells the therapist about the events that occurred in a dream. The therapist then helps to uncover the meaning of the dream, which was previously hidden in the depths of the unconscious mind.

Psychoanalytic therapy involves clarifying, confronting, interpreting, and working through one's issues. Through the therapeutic strategies discussed, the client learns to develop *insight* into her personality, defective coping strategies, and dysfunctional and destructive behaviors.

Traditional psychoanalysis tends to work best for clients who are intelligent, stable, and old enough to be able to develop insight and learn from it. Many therapists work from a *psychodynamic orientation*. This means that the basic theoretical framework and strategies used are primarily derived from psychoanalysis and then modified.

Humanistic Psychotherapies

Other clinical psychotherapies include but are not limited to *Client-Centered Therapy, Reality Therapy,* and *Existential Therapy.* Each of these stems from a theory of personality of how psychopathology and dysfunctional behaviors develop, and how each makes use of specific therapy techniques. There is considerable overlap among theories and strategies, which are derived primarily from psychodynamic therapy and expanded, modified, and/or diversified.

Client-Centered Therapy, developed by Carl Rogers, helps the client become a more fully functioning, whole, and self-actualizing person. The theory is that people learn to regard themselves in much the same way they experience regard from others, especially in terms of liking or disliking themselves. The more "conditional" a parent's love is (for example, Mother will love you only if you act in a certain way, look a certain way, or accomplish certain things), the more likely psychopathology, a distorted sense of self, and low self-esteem are to develop. The therapist provides a "corrective emotional experience" by providing and communicating accurate empathic understanding, genuineness, and unconditional positive regard (total acceptance) of the client, the way that parents or primary caretakers should have, thus affirming the client's worth as a person—simply because she is a person. In time, the client learns to internalize this experience, to mature emotionally, and to grow as a person. The therapeutic relationship is seen as the primary curative factor and of utmost importance.

The goal of *Reality Therapy,* founded by William Glasser, is to help the client become *responsible* and thus develop a "success" identity. This type of therapy is verbally active, intellectual, and involves the use of confrontation. The theory is that most forms of emotional disturbance and mental illness reflect the person's own irresponsibility, which results in a "failure identity." The focus is on present behaviors, not on unconscious conflicts or on past experiences. The client is to realize and actively confront what is wrong in her daily life and take action and fix it by applying specific behaviors.

In *Existential Therapy*, the therapist helps the client achieve an *authentic* existence, or mode of being in the world. The personality is an emerging, a becoming, a process of being. Certain conditions in existence will tempt people to run from too much awareness. Lying to and about ourselves in relationship to other people is considered the foundation of psychopathology, which leads to neurotic anxiety. To relieve symptoms, one must become honest with oneself and with others.

The therapist does not use any actual therapeutic techniques, but rather helps the client become more aware of her own being-in-the-world. This is accomplished by developing authenticity through self-disclosure and by the therapist modeling authentic behaviors. The client is supposed to say whatever he or she wants to say. This is called "free experiencing," much like Freud's free association. The therapist uses clarification and feedback. Confrontation is also used. Here, the therapist provides the client with a genuine reaction. For example, the therapist may state bluntly: "You're the most rotten, obnoxious kid I ever met!" The client becomes conscious of alternatives and makes choices—and takes responsibility for choices. The therapist supports the client during critical choice points in therapy, where the client decides whether or not to risk a fundamental aspect of existence (for example, to get married right after high school or to go away to college and get a degree first). The therapeutic relationship is an equal one, and is considered the curative factor. The therapist does not play the role of a doctor or a parent, but instead uses confrontation of issues and enables the client to make her own choices.

Behavior Therapy

Behavior Therapy, which stems from the work of B. F. Skinner and learning theory, is a diverse system of therapy with many different techniques. The goal is changing behavior. Conditions or situations in the environment are considered to have greater influence in controlling behavior than do internal personality traits and conflicts. Behavior therapies are intended to be short-term and practical treatments.

In Behavior Therapy, counter-conditioning techniques, contingency management techniques, and cognitive techniques are used.

The theory of psychopathology behind *counter-conditioning techniques* is that anxiety is the key to most behavior disorders. Anxiety can be learned through conditioning. For example, when Joan has anxiety whenever she sees a dog, it has to do with her previous experience of being bitten by a dog. The response is generalized. Anxiety may produce secondary symptoms like ulcers or colitis. Successful treatment calls for elimination of a specific anxiety response. Systematic desensitization deals with teaching the client to behave in a method that is inconsistent with anxiety while in the presence (real or imagined) of the anxiety-evoking stimulus (which, for Joan, is dogs). This method is primarily used in the treatment of phobias.

Another counter-conditioning technique used in Behavior Therapy is *assertiveness training.* This is used to treat anxieties related to interactions with other people. Being assertive and feeling anxiety are incompatible. The therapist teaches and models direct and effective verbal responses for specific social situations. Clients are encouraged to practice new and appropriate assertive responses. This is done through role-playing with the therapist and by imagining being more assertive in situations where they were previously inhibited (for example, in conversations with an unreasonable boss who has a dictator-like attitude). The client is given feedback by the therapist and becomes more self-confident in facing real-life situations. Assertiveness training also takes place in group therapy and in training seminars that are available to the general public and to specific groups of people such as business professionals.

The theory behind *contingency management techniques* is that behavior is largely controlled by its consequences. Dysfunctional behaviors will decrease if they are not rewarded. Reinforcements and punishments that are made contingent on particular responses can affect maladaptive behavior patterns and affect the development of new responses.

For example, an alcoholic/addict self-injuring teenager in a group home for adolescents on court probation may earn privileges such as extended home passes or being able to go on outings such as fun trips to Disneyland (positive reinforcement). These rewards are given if she remains clean and sober, does not self-injure, goes to school, and has good behavior. However, if she misbehaves, such as by sneaking alcohol or drugs into the home and getting the other girls to use along with her, she will go back to juvenile hall (punishment).

Behavioral problems that are frequently addressed and respond well to contingency management techniques include deficits in responding (for example, rarely socializing with other people), excesses in responding (for example, overeating or compulsive hair-pulling), and inappropriate responding (for example, having emotional outbursts when angry at other people).

There are a variety of contingency management techniques that can be used, depending on the person and the situation. For example, token economies are frequently used in mental institutions. Here, appropriate behaviors are rewarded with tangible reinforcers (such as poker chips) that can later be exchanged for desired objects or privileges. Or, therapists can provide clients with verbal positive reinforcement ("Great job; you are getting better!"). Sometimes *contracting* is used in therapy, where an agreement is written and signed by both parties (the therapist and the client). *Aversion therapy* is a form of punishment that involves the removal of positive reinforcers or the use of aversive stimuli (for example, electric shocks—which are controversial under any circumstances, and most definitely should not be used for self-injurers!). Covert sensitization involves conditioning through covert stimuli such as thoughts and images (for example, a child molester is to imagine vomiting when looking at a little kid).

Cognitive-Behavioral Techniques combine mental cognitions (thoughts and ideas) and behaviors. The goal is for the client to understand why she behaves in a certain way, the cause-and-effect nature of the behaviors, and how thoughts can influence behaviors. The client learns how to actively change negative thoughts and ideas and the dysfunctional behaviors that go along with them.

Some dysfunctional behaviors reflect a deficit in cognitive activity—that is, the person does not think before acting. Or, sometimes a cognition may occur repeatedly and unnecessarily (for example, obsessive thoughts about drinking or using, or excessive worrying about a situation that one has little or no control over). Sometimes people have developed ineffective problem-solving strategies.

The therapist works with the client by providing the information necessary to gain cognitive control over dysfunctional behaviors, through increased awareness. The client learns how to, first of all, define and formulate the problem, then to see the consequences, and then to generate alternative behaviors.

Group Therapy

Group therapy is an increasingly popular form of psychotherapy. The dynamics of shared experience and learning from others can be extremely powerful and produce many long-term benefits. Additionally, group as opposed to individual therapy is more economical and more feasible time-wise for the clients, the therapists, and the treatment settings in which they operate.

Nearly every approach to psychotherapy has been applied to group therapy. Groups vary greatly in terms of theoretical orientation and strategies that are used, in their treatment goals, and in the settings in which they occur. Group therapists' views of personality and of what causes maladaptive behavior depend on their theoretical orientation and training (for example, psychodynamic or behavioral). However, group therapists generally believe that abnormal behavior is in at least some way related to dysfunctional social relationships with other people.

Client characteristics of groups can be either similar or different. Working in therapy with similar groups of people is especially effective for certain problems such as alcoholism, substance abuse, depression, rape and sexual abuse, and chronic illnesses (such as groups for children with juvenile diabetes). For example, Elaine, a thirty-five-year-old self-injurer and compulsive overeater, found it very helpful to attend a group for women survivors of childhood incest, led by a trained therapist who had been there herself. For the first time in her life, she felt understood and not alone.

Groups that are more "mixed" tend to promote more dynamic group interaction and long-lasting positive change. People can learn how to better get along with others who are different from themselves and can learn how to compromise. They can see things from a variety of different perspectives and can incorporate ideas that they would not have come up with on their own or with a similar group of people.

The therapist's job is primarily to facilitate and monitor the group process. A number of different strategies can be used. Groups for adolescents in residential treatment centers, for example, give everyone a chance to share and provide feedback to their peers. Many times these groups tend to focus on accountability for oneself as well as for others in the program, from a positive peer-pressure model. The therapist and co-therapists give their input and perceptions of situations, as well as provide direction, guidance, coming to emotional resolution, and teaching of problem-solving skills.

Other groups, for example, use a model wherein each person shares on a particular topic that is proposed for discussion, such as the loss of a loved one or a recent crisis. The sharing is brief, usually three to five minutes. The therapist monitors the time and keeps order. The others in the group remain silent, thus not giving verbal feedback or cross talk (that is, no commenting on another person's share). This allows group members to openly share their thoughts and feelings in a mutually supportive atmosphere. This model is frequently used in large groups, for example, in school crisis situations where a consulting therapist/ trauma expert is flown in to work with large groups of students and teachers who have been affected (for example, the Columbine and San Diego high school shootings).

According to Yalom (1985), renowned expert and author on group therapy, all types of therapy groups provide their members with a number of "curative factors." These include but are not limited to *emotional catharsis,* which is the expression of strong feelings and receiving support and acceptance from others regarding those feelings; *interpersonal learning,* where members learn to identify and change their maladaptive ways of relating to others through having interactions with others in a safe, mutually supportive setting; and *altruism,* where group members have opportunities to learn that they are capable of helping others (for example, by giving moral support and helpful feedback), which in turn increases their own self-esteem and sense of worth.

Family Therapy

Family therapy is the therapy of families. It attempts to modify the relationships in a family to achieve harmony. The focus is on the family system as a whole, rather than on one person as the identified patient. The interactions between the marital and sibling subsystems result in *homeostasis,* or balance, within a family. All systems operate within given limits. When the limits are crossed, or the rules are broken, difficulty results. If the difficulty cannot be corrected, the system will fall apart.

The family therapist's work is to change relationships between members of the family so that symptomatic (dysfunctional) behavior disappears. The primary goal is to produce overt behavior change, whether or not the family is aware of what is happening. Changes in behavior are considered evidence of progress. Changes in thinking and feelings are considered far less important.

Traditional behavior-modification techniques, such as

positive and negative reinforcement, are used to treat a particular problem (for example, attention deficit disorder in a child) but with the family therapist viewing and addressing the problem as affected by, and also affecting, the interactions within the family system (for example, parents who are frustrated and inconsistent with appropriate discipline).

Some family therapists believe that the clients' symptoms (for example, an anorexic daughter, an alcoholic father) are both the cause and effect of dysfunctional communications and interactions in the family. By learning how to more effectively communicate with one another, behaviors change and symptoms improve. The therapist analyzes the faulty communication patterns and interactions, and acts as a teacher or director. For example, the therapist can instruct the family members to use "I" statements (for example, "I feel scared when you get drunk and smash things, Dad") instead of making accusatory statements or talking "at" people or about them to others when they are right there in the room.

Reënactment is a technique in which the therapist asks the family members to act out a situation in the therapy session instead of just giving an example. For instance, a mother and teenage daughter have difficulty communicating and basically do not get along. The therapist will ask them to have a conversation about an issue they disagree on (for example, the daughter's pink hair or choice of older, objectionable boyfriends). This results in a tearful, loud, and heated argument between the two. The therapist analyzes the interaction, points out what is wrong, and helps by fostering better communication skills.

Family Sculpting is a therapeutic technique by which the magnitude of closeness and power are examined in a nonverbal way. For example, a child who is seen as the family scapegoat may be asked to describe his place in the family not by using words, but by using space. He moves his chair away from the others and faces the wall.

A family therapist may work with the family in constructing a *genogram,* a structural diagram drawn on paper that illustrates the generational relationship system. This typically includes the grandparents on both sides, the parents, and their children. Members of the extended family may also be included, depending on how in-depth an analysis is undertaken. Interpersonal relationships, relevant events, boundaries and other important data are landmarked (for example, marriage, divorce, death, imprisonment, alcoholism, estrangement between family members).

Paradoxical Interventions are frequently used by strategic family therapists, who take an active, directive role and use particular strategies that are designed to prevent the repetition of dysfunctional behaviors. For example, a married couple who frequently argue are given a directive by the therapist to go home and argue for at least two hours every night. The hope is that the couple will resist the therapist's request, seeing how ridiculous it is, and that they will stop arguing.

Multi-family groups are a therapeutic technique in which several families are seen at one time in a large group. These groups are quite powerful and dynamic. Most people enjoy coming to them, are motivated, and tend to get a lot out of each group session.

Multi-family groups usually consist of parents and children (who are old enough to participate and to not be disruptive) and sometimes extended family members, such as a grandparent, aunt, or uncle, who are relevant in the identified patient's life. Typically, two therapists (oftentimes, a male and a female) lead the group. Most of these groups take place in hospital inpatient and residential treatment settings, wherein the identified patients' relevant issues are the focus of attention. For example, one of the multi-family groups I ran along with a co-therapist several years ago was on an adolescent eating disorders unit in a community hospital, where teens and their parents discussed issues and family dynamics related to anorexia, bulimia, and compulsive overeating.

The particular benefits of multi-family groups are that people can relate to others who are in the same situation. For example, frustrated parents can talk with other frustrated parents who are dealing with acting-out teenagers. They can truly understand, empathize, and feel like they are not the only ones in the world dealing with a problem. With the direction and guidance of the therapists, group members learn from and help each other. Family dynamics and issues surface and are confronted directly in group. All members have a chance to participate and give feedback, not only to their own family members but also to others.

Psychopharmacology

Psychopharmacological intervention is when prescription medications are used to treat emotionally based disorders. Cases of severe depression and debilitating anxiety may be particularly amenable to this type of treatment. The use of psychotropic medications usually occurs in conjunction with clinical psychotherapy.

Psychotropic medications are prescribed by a licensed physician, who is usually a psychiatrist. A psychologist, social worker, or other mental health professional is typically the one who makes the referral for evaluation, but does not make recommendations. Psychiatrists sometimes provide medication consultations exclusively, with an initial diagnostic session and brief (sometimes fifteen-minute) follow-up sessions at designated time periods and also on an as-needed basis. Some psychiatrists also provide traditional clinical psychotherapy.

Twelve Step and Other Mutual-Help Groups

Twelve Step groups such as Alcoholics Anonymous and Overeaters Anonymous are the most popular and readily available support groups in the community. They help many people attain and maintain abstinence and progress along the road to recovery. The various types of Twelve Step groups, the most well-known and popular ones, are individually described in detail in chapter 8. There are other mutual help groups, some with and some without a spiritual focus. Many religious organizations such as local churches have support groups that are specifically for recovering alcoholics and addicts. Recovery groups without a spiritual focus, for those who are not interested in that aspect of it or who are turned off by the mention of "God," are also an option.

Mutual-help groups are not "group therapy" or a form of clinical treatment. They are composed of general people in the community who want to recover from alcoholism and/or other addictions themselves and who want to offer help and moral support to others. In most, such as in Twelve Step groups, there are no leaders or directors. There are no dues or fees; however, members may pass a basket around for small donations (usually pocket change or a dollar, but they don't care whether you contribute or not) to help cover the cost of the meeting room rental, literature, and coffee and cookies.

Clinical therapists often recommend Twelve Step and other mutual help groups as an adjunct to therapy. However, attending meetings or talking to a program sponsor is by no means a "substitute" for clinical treatment. These groups can, nevertheless, provide constant support and contact with other members, both in person and by exchanging telephone numbers, as well as readily available safe places to go and people to develop new social friendships with— which is not in the framework of what therapists can provide.

Stress-Reduction Strategies and Biofeedback

Biofeedback is a popular relaxation technique that teaches clients to become aware of and to control their body responses. Electrical monitors record heart rate, blood pressure, skin temperature, and brain waves. This can decrease emotional stress and anxiety and promote relaxation, as well as promote physical pain relief. Meditation techniques are sometimes incorporated. Biofeedback is usually administered by a physician or a psychologist.

Numerous studies have shown that meditation, deep-breathing exercises, relaxation tapes, yoga, and *guided imagery* (when one visualizes pleasant environments or positive outcomes) are beneficial. These techniques decrease stress and anxiety, promote a general feeling of well being, help create an inner calm, promote endorphin release, and decrease physical pain and muscle tension. Prayer, meditation, and quiet contemplation are also very powerful.

In summary, there are a number of different treatment options and approaches available to self-injurers, alcoholics and other addicts, and others who are experiencing emotional distress. If one does not seem to be working right away, give it a fair chance. Overnight "miracle cures" should not be expected. Also, the client/patient should remember to trust her own intuition. If needed, other options (for example, a different type of treatment or therapy, or a different therapist) should be explored.

Why Treatment Often Fails

Treatment for the problem of self-injury tends to fail, unfortunately, more often than not. There are a number of reasons for this. First, most people, even trained mental health professionals with many years of experience, do not fully understand the dynamics of self-injury. The clinical literature is scarce. Only a minimal amount of helpful information, especially on treating the problem, has been imparted to professionals or to the general public.

The most common response from other clinicians, including doctoral-level psychologists, school and mental health professionals who have master's degrees, and medical doctors is something like: "What? Self-injury? I never heard of it . . . oh yeah, I have seen a couple of teenagers who cut their wrists but who didn't really want to kill themselves, and I wondered why they did it . . . and there was something about it on *20/20* awhile back." If asked, most people in general find that they personally know, or at least know about, one or two people (usually teenage girls or women) who currently have or who have had the problem of self-injury.

Research on the problem of self-injury is now predominantly in the "admiring disorders" phase. This means that clinicians and researchers are mostly focused on coming up with definitions, hypothetical explanations for why it happens, and statistical correlations with other factors such as child abuse and post-traumatic stress disorder. It is now time to stop merely "admiring disorders" and figure out what to *do* about treatment. The time for this is long over-due for the problem of self-injury.

Another reason why treatment for self-injury often fails is because many therapists are squeamish and/or afraid to treat this problem. They may be taken aback by the sight of blood or think that the client will kill herself, either acciden-tally or on purpose. Liability issues might also be of concern. Feelings of inadequacy, frustration, or guilt might haunt therapists when trying to help self-injurers, especially when their clients relapse. Most clients, especially children, ado-lescents, and alcoholics and addicts who are more sensitive, usually do sense their therapist's discomfort. Feeling misun-derstood or unwanted by others is one of the most painful emotions in human experience. This can be particularly detrimental in therapy, because the therapeutic relationship is a magnified relationship. In turn, many clients/patients do not come back and may give up on seeking therapy altogether.

Most important, treatment for self-injury often fails be-cause the approaches that are used, although well inten-tioned, are just plain wrong. This is primarily because there is not yet a clear-cut theoretical framework to work from. As described in chapter 2, self-injury can be seen as an ad-dictive process, much like alcoholism, drug addiction, and other behavioral addictions. Therefore, similar treatment options can be applied and modified for self-injury addicts as well.

Too Much Too Soon

Many therapists are not aware or do not understand the problem of self-injury from an addictions perspective. Therefore, issues such as child sexual abuse and trauma, which are too painful for the newly recovering addict to deal with, are brought up way too quickly, before the addict is actually stable and strong enough to deal with the emotional pain. In the very beginning of recovery, the addict feels emotionally raw and ripped open anyway, with no more anesthetic to numb the great pain of life. Bringing up the repressed trauma too soon can feel like someone (the therapist, who is supposed to be helping) is reaching deeper in, trying to wrench one's guts out with a crowbar. The struggling client, who is still emotionally fragile, will most likely resist, become angry, and attempt to run away. This may be further exacerbated by the therapist's (sometimes overzealous) desire to "fix" things and to be helpful, instead of being able to truly "be there" in a supportive manner.

Some self-injurers may be very anxious to get better and are willing to work hard in therapy. However, it is important not to overdo it. Attempting to resurface memories before one is ready and talking too soon about emotionally traumatic issues can be dangerous. This can lead to relapse. The guideline is to proceed with caution. The therapist needs to monitor the process. The self-injurer needs to, first and foremost, be committed to abstinence and to have attained some time in recovery. She must then be able to slow down, stabilize, and sit with and simply "be" with the uncomfortable internal sensations and emotions for a while.

Keys to Successful Treatment

First, Eliminate the Symptom

As with any addiction, first, the "symptom" (that is, the act of drinking alcohol, using drugs, or slashing and burning) must be eliminated. *Abstinence* from the substance or the self-destructive behavior is absolutely necessary before beginning to tackle deep-rooted emotional issues.

Finding a Therapist—Things to Look For

Finding a therapist who is competent and knowledgeable in treating complex trauma and self-injury, whom the client feels comfortable with, is most beneficial. However, this is not always possible. Choices may be limited for low-income clients who can only go to community mental health centers or county clinics with long waiting lists and very brief treatments. No matter what therapeutic approach and strategy the therapist uses, or whether the therapist is in a private-practice setting or in a community clinic, it is important that he or she is a stable, "calm, cool, and collected" type of person who has a positive attitude and inspires hope. An ideal therapist for a chronic self-injurer is one who is supportive, warm, and nurturing, who knows how to respond effectively rather than react to the client's crises and emotional outbursts. The therapist should also be firm, directive, not easily manipulated, and capable of breaking through the addict's denial system. There are benefits to seeing a therapist who has many years of experience and acquired wisdom from "having seen a lot of things" in working with clients, even if not directly related to the problem of self-injury.

Therapists who are addicts themselves with long-term recovery tend to work exceptionally well with clients who are struggling with addictions of any type, including self-injury. They truly understand, because they have been there themselves. They can be inspiring, positive role models. After all, they offer hope because they have come through the battle successfully.

CHAPTER SEVEN

Addressing the Spiritual Void

Spirituality is an abstract, intangible concept that is hard to define, hard to put into words. Furthermore, because the process of becoming spiritual is such an individualized experience, it may mean somewhat different things to different people. A Catholic priest who is in a Twelve Step program defined spirituality as "a call to be in relationship with God or a Higher Power, and a willingness to share that grace with others." *Grace* is the unmerited Divine assistance given to us for our realization of, or being restored to, a better, higher, or more worthy state.

Religious versus Spiritual

There is a major difference between being "religious" and being spiritual. Spirituality goes *beyond* religiously or zealously adhering to a set of required observances, rules, or attendance at church services. It is a *process* that involves thought and exploration, time and work. It is genuine, and it is a product of our own internal awareness.

Author Marsha Sinetar describes the concept of genuine spirituality and internal awareness, which also applies to those who do not belong to an organized religion, very well in her book *Ordinary People as Monks and Mystics: Lifestyles for Self-Discovery* (1986):

> [F]or socially transcendent persons there isn't someone "out there" (i.e., in the home, organization, community, or church) telling them to be obedient to this rule or that policy. Rather it is they themselves who desire something more, who desire the goals their inner self only vaguely whispers. These individuals learn to listen carefully to their inner authority as a way of saving their integrity and their very lives.

At about four years into my recovery, I was in the process of writing the proposal for this book. I was initially going to include the concept of spirituality only briefly and incidentally. After hearing many stories of self-injurers, alcoholics, and addicts struggling through and progressing with their recovery, I decided that it is worth a whole chapter.

To most effectively recover from self-injury or any other addiction—be it from alcoholism, drug addiction, or some other type of compulsive behavioral addiction—three areas need to be addressed throughout recovery. These are the physical, emotional, and spiritual sides of recovery.

Think of it as a three-legged stool, where each side is absolutely necessary for it to be fully functional and stable. If one of the legs is broken or missing, it will not work. If one of the legs is shaky, the whole piece of furniture can collapse.

The self-injurer, just like an alcoholic or addict, can collapse if one of the sides is broken, shaky, or missing.

The Physical and Emotional Sides of Recovery

It may be necessary—even essential—to address an addict's physical issues first in the beginning stages of recovery. An example of this would be when a severe alcoholic is going through the detoxification process, or when a heroin addict is going through the process of physical withdrawal, or when a self-injurer has a life-threatening injury or a severely infected wound that requires medical treatment.

Emotional issues tend to come up and predominate next. Feelings such as anger, rage, anxiety, paranoia, frustration, grief, and/or deep sadness are common. Frequently, the addict has become an expert in running away from, or may never have dealt with, these feelings at all. Once the addict becomes abstinent, there is no more anesthetic to numb the pain of life. The ever-present temptation to run back to the addictive behavior or substance is there.

For example, the self-injurer may be at a stage in her recovery where she is beginning to deal with her childhood abuse and trauma issues in therapy. If she is not yet strong enough to deal with these issues and especially if she does not have a readily available social support system (such as family or friends) after the therapy hour is over, she may in desperation turn to self-injury, alcohol, or drugs for comfort.

Dealing with the emotional and physical aspects of recovery can be tough. To effectively deal with all of this, the self-injurer needs something to grasp onto to avoid completely falling apart. The self-injury addict often feels left there, all alone, with nothing more to turn to. People who are not alcoholics or recovering addicts themselves just don't seem to understand. It's common for family, romantic partners, friends, and acquaintances to abandon the sufferer when things get tough. Even the wonderful people who really care and can handle it, although many times very helpful and well intentioned, cannot always be there 100 percent of the time. Even the most reliable people can come down with the flu or have car problems, sometimes when they are needed most.

The self-injurer needs to learn to no longer be dependent, be it on a substance or a compulsive behavior, nor unhealthily dependent on other people.

So what else is there? To help them in their recovery process, many people explore their spirituality. People who already have some sort of a positive spiritual or religious foundation through their childhood upbringing are at an advantage. The whole process of recovery will be made easier from the very beginning when spirituality is already a part of their lives.

The Spiritual Side of Recovery

The majority of people today—whether addicts or nonaddicts—are "searching for something." Problems of poverty, illness, abuse, violence, and all types of other unfairnesses abound. There is a deep sense of longing within all of us, in every human being, be it conscious or unconscious, that cries out for a sense of meaning, of wholeness, and of connectedness with some Power greater than ourselves. Many addicts, including self-injurers, describe chronic feelings of emptiness.

At some time in their lives, most people feel some degree of emptiness. They may also describe this as a feeling of being alone in the world; or as sense of inadequacy, or ineffectiveness, or insufficiency; or as a lack of meaning in their lives. Some may describe this as a spiritual longing.

Unfortunately, it is quite often that people are brought to this point of internal contemplation via some sort of personal tragedy. Many people contemplate God and life when someone close to them dies or when they themselves have a brush with death, be it through a physical illness, an accident or injury, or through the downfall of their addiction. Some may just look around and decide that life is unfair and ask themselves the question "Why?"

Years ago, the renowned Swiss psychiatrist Carl Jung described the concept of a thirst of our soul for wholeness, for the union with God, as a fundamental human drive that has great power in our lives. This deep drive to know our true self summons a state of unrest or spiritual discontent, of searching for something Divine, and of a need to become whole. In a letter to Bill Wilson, the cofounder of Alcoholics Anonymous, Dr. Jung described one of his patients: "His craving for alcohol was the equivalent on a low level of the spiritual thirst of our being for wholeness, expressed in medieval language: the union with God" (Grof 1993).

The words *whole, holy,* and *heal* all contain a deep and constant similarity; they bring forth the idea that wholeness and healing are related. The true purpose and meaning of each life *is* to become whole or complete. This is the driving point of our existence as human beings. Self-injurers, alcoholics, and addicts must become whole, and on some level spiritual, to be healed.

The place of wholeness that we seek exists within our deepest self, which can be described as our spiritual core. The intense and sometimes excruciatingly painful craving to fill the emptiness with something, sometimes with almost anything, is actually a deep hunger or thirst for our own wholeness, for our true spiritual identity and awareness, and for our Divine source from whence we came.

However, this strong impulse, or hunger within, sometimes becomes distorted and misdirected. It may be because spirituality is difficult to understand or that one does not know how to fill the void in an appropriate way.

Many people try to fill the chronic internal emptiness in

unhealthy ways. Alcohol, drugs, self-injury and other self-destructive behaviors, compulsive sexual acting-out, or all-consuming (usually destructive) interpersonal relationships are sometimes used to fill the void.

Some people may actually be unconsciously, subconsciously, or even consciously searching for a spiritual connection of some sort and mistakenly think that they found it through the feeling that comes on by being artificially high.

There are definite dangers to searching for a spiritual connection by using addictive substances like alcohol and drugs, and to indulging in addictive behaviors, especially those like self-injury, that cause physiological reactions within the body. The first and most obvious danger is the devastation to the body, the mind, and the central nervous system. It may even lead to overdose or death, because the user is in an artificial state of bliss and out of control. At the very least, the addict may become so lethargic and brain-dead that he cannot have the spiritual experience that was sought.

It is frequently reported in the media that certain rock stars, musicians, and movie stars have had problems with alcohol and drugs. Some do not make it—their substance of choice kills them. Others have gone into recovery, and when they make their comeback, their work and their fame are greater than ever before.

When the problem of self-injury becomes very serious, the sufferer may come to think that she needs her high in order to be at her best and, finally, merely to keep on functioning. The end results are the same as for alcohol and for drugs.

Alcoholics and addicts often talk about a deeper craving, a longing for something more, that remains when they stop using their addictive substance or substances of choice. The physical craving is gone. They are now faced with their own utter aloneness.

Most people have a hard time finding the right words to describe the feelings of chronic emptiness deep inside. Addicted adolescents in particular frequently talk about feeling "bored" when they are beginning to approach the point of being able to identify and address the spiritual void.

In a clinical therapy session several years ago at a residential treatment facility for teenage boys on court probation, a seventeen-year-old boy who was severely alcoholic, multi-drug addicted, and gang affiliated (and who also had a destructive compulsion with making homemade tattoos) stated: "Okay, so I gave up the alcohol and drugs and everything, so what else is there? My life is empty; there ain't nothin' else."

Jose was at a point in his recovery when he was just beginning to scratch the surface of facing and addressing the spiritual void, the emptiness within, getting to his inner core, his truest self. He eventually became motivated to find some sense of "meaning" and purpose in his life. Jose was able to do so successfully, with the help of an excellent social worker who had been there himself. Jose began to help the other boys in the residential facility (his "homeboys") to give up alcohol and drugs. This brought him a sense of meaning, of wholeness, of completeness, and of purpose to his life.

Some people may become inappropriately focused on and even addicted to such things as acquiring material possessions, money, power, or prestige. In this sense, and when taken to an extreme, these things become increasingly artificial and ultimately insufficient. The feelings of internal emptiness only become magnified.

There was an interesting study that was broadcast on the early morning radio news in Los Angeles a few years ago. The study measured the levels of happiness between paraplegics and millionaire lottery winners. Guess who was happier? The paraplegics, and it was statistically significant.

This was because the paraplegics had endured a physical tragedy, survived, and thus became genuinely spiritual on some level through their gratitude. They were truly happy to be alive.

Others may choose to completely ignore their spiritual potential, even to disown that part of themselves. They are reluctant to look deep within or reluctant to face the fact that in order to grow, change must take place. Taking the path of least resistance, of avoiding spiritual awareness and growth, may somehow look easier.

All addictions, attempts at artificial highs, and avoidance will eventually backfire.

Marcus, a social worker who works with addicted teenagers (who himself had a problem with compulsive overeating), was going through a phase of intense spiritual contemplation, right after his divorce from his wife. He said to one of his co-workers: "If you make anything more important than God—whether it is alcohol, drugs, food, or anything else, even a relationship—you will eventually lose it, or it will backfire."

Brother Paul, a Benedictine monk, stated in one of his sermons: "Anything that leads you away from God, or that becomes more important than God, or that doesn't lead you to God, must go." He then explained, using his own words and referring to Scripture, that this could include such things as alcohol, power, and money, and that virtually any vice that gets in the way must be removed from a person's life.

Child Abuse, Trauma, and God

Our first experience with a Higher Power is Mom and Dad. Parents or parent figures are the people whom a child is initially dependent on, who take care of him or her, who appear to be all-powerful, and whom the child looks up to in adoration. If a parent or guardian is a negative role model to a child, such as with children who have been abused, the whole concept of God becomes convoluted. It is hard to relate to "God the Loving Father" (or father figure) if your own father was an alcoholic who beat you. And forget about "Mother Church" if your own mother wasn't there to protect you.

A child victim of incest may not even be able to fathom a concept of God as a benevolent figure or as one who is all-powerful. She may ask herself the questions, on a subconscious level and not in so many words: "How can there possibly be a God? If there really was one, how could he let something so horrible happen to me? Or maybe he forgot about me?"

It may be especially difficult for those who self-injure to connect with a concept of God or a Higher Power or religion. Self-injurers typically have horrendous histories of childhood physical abuse, sexual abuse, or neglect. Some have had severe traumatic experiences as an adolescent or as an adult, such as rape. Being able to turn to, let alone trust, anyone at all often seems out of the question for self-injurers. This is also true for many alcoholics and other addicts while in the throes of their addiction, as well as in the beginning stages of recovery.

The self-injurer has issues of needing to be in control, completely self-reliant, and "tougher than life." She needs to develop a more positive approach and to consider how she can change her way of thinking.

The only way to get rid of bad ideas about God is to go out and get some new ones. One can read, talk to other people, or search for meaning or a belief system that may or may not include becoming affiliated with a particular organized religion.

Father Ron, a Jesuit priest and an alcoholic with long-term recovery, was able to constructively change his way of thinking through a lot of deep contemplation. He described his original concept of God as "distant and far-off, like my father was." He now says that the things he believes about God are that "God is intelligent; God is skillful; God is compassionate and wishes me well."

A Higher Power

Many addicts, including self-injurers, are resistant to, or may not be able to focus on—or even to acknowledge—that there may be "something" out there that is bigger and better and more powerful than themselves and their Almighty Addiction. This is especially true for most people who are still struggling with their addiction or who are in the very beginning stages of recovery. The addiction has become *the* most important and *the* most powerful thing in the person's life. But there is something better.

As stated in the Big Book of Alcoholics Anonymous (1976) in the appendix on spiritual experience:

> With few exceptions many of our members find that they have tapped an unsuspected inner resource which they presently identify with their own conception of a Power greater than themselves. Most of us think this awareness of a Power greater than ourselves is the essence of spiritual experience. Our more religious members call it "God-consciousness."

To become spiritual, alcoholics and addicts must first become *willing, ready,* and then *able* to surrender to the idea that there is Something bigger, better, and more powerful than themselves or their addiction—Something that is positive and that won't let them down.

The addict is likely, at least initially, to be almost

completely self-absorbed, with grandiose and defective thinking (although he or she may not think so!). The addict has a sense of total personal involvement with, and adoration of, drinking, using drugs, and/or repetitively engaging in some other type of self-destructive compulsive behavior.

Being caught in the vicious cycle of addictive behavior, the addict will eventually hit bottom and is at the mercy of a destructive force that is bigger than one's self. The addict eventually goes completely out of control and arrives at a "crossroads" where her whole being intuitively knows that it's not working anymore, that her life is not working anymore, and that the addiction has finally defeated her. All defenses, denial, and resistances collapse. The all-encompassing and overwhelming power of the Almighty Addiction gives way and opens the door to Something better, Something more positive and healing and Divine, if she is willing, ready, and able to surrender.

The addict then needs to eventually become able to view this more positive force as more desirable, and ultimately more important, than the addictive substance or behavior or the "high" that results from the addiction.

Some may call this God. Or a Higher Power. Or Allah. Or Buddha. Or nature. Or the power of the Universe. Or the sum total of all that is good.

Surrendering to some sort of a Higher Power is indeed possible for those who are not religious. Some may choose to see this as the Higher Power of their particular Twelve Step group (for example, Alcoholics Anonymous, Cocaine Anonymous, or Overeaters Anonymous) or as the Higher Power of their Twelve Step program as a whole.

Some may have a conception of a Higher Power as "the greater needs of humanity" or as having a primary focus on putting first, and being of help and service to, those who are less fortunate than themselves.

There are many different roads to and ways of thinking about spirituality. There are many routes to accomplishing the same thing. There is no one and only "right" way to proceed along a spiritual path.

Many addicts—including self-injurers—recover through addressing their spirituality, distinctly or in connection with other types of treatment. Many attend spiritually based programs such as Twelve Step groups. Others turn to religion for the first time in their lives or return to their church, temple, or synagogue after long absences, which may have been since early childhood. Prayer, meditation, belief in God or a Higher Power, and helping others often become a very important part of a recovering addict's life and are seen as important, if not essential, to long-term recovery.

Spiritual Awakening

Spiritual awakening is a term that is frequently used, especially in Twelve Step programs, to describe a specific yet very abstract and esoteric concept. It is the realization of, the absolute knowing—for sure and without a doubt in one's mind—that there is Something great and Divine in the universe. This realization may happen in a profound moment or through a process over a period of time.

My spiritual awakening was primarily of the long-term educational variety. At a little over two years into my recovery, I unexpectedly had one of those profound experiences.

Here's what happened: My appendix exploded. It was initially hard for the doctors to diagnose, and it seemed to take forever, until an MRI revealed what was wrong. However, by this time, I was slowly being poisoned by peritonitis. They put me on heavy-duty antibiotics for a while before attempting the necessary surgery, because at this point, it had become very risky. I asked the surgeon during a medical consultation whether or not I was going to survive this thing, and he gave me a very surprising response: "Maybe, if you believe in God or a Higher Power or something. Here at this hospital, they have these posters all over the place that say 'Saint John's . . . Answering to a Higher Power. Believe it.' Most hospitals have posters that say things like 'We Have the Greatest Doctors in the World.'"

A few days later when I was ready to go under the knife, as the anesthesia was going through me and I was being wheeled down the seemingly endless hospital hallways, I kept seeing that poster over and over again . . . the last thing I remember before going into surgery were the words *Believe it.*

Because I happened to be doing the "ninety meetings in ninety days" as recommended in the AA program (that was one thing I never did in the beginning of my recovery and now had time to do), I was upset about making it to only eighty-nine days. I decided that if I survived the surgery, I might somehow make it to ninety later on that day, if I went to a Twelve Step meeting on the Internet.

As I was beginning to wake up from the anesthesia after the surgery in my hospital room, I kept hearing the words *Big Book, AA, God.* There was an AA meeting going on right there in my hospital room! Carla, my roommate, was in the AA program. Her husband and a group of three or four of their friends came to gather for a meeting, because she could not physically get to one. She was a sweet yet tough-appearing Harley-Davidson biker girl, with a tattoo of the AA circle and triangle on her arm. Later on that afternoon, she told me that she had been walking around the hospital for the last five days, showing off her tattoo, asking people, "Any friends of Bill around here?" She could not find anybody in the AA program. I told her about my addiction and recovery, and she said to me, "Wow! How lucky can you be? You get wheeled right into an AA meeting right after surgery!" We stayed up talking and watching old sitcoms on TV all night. Carla shared with me that she was alcoholic, bulimic, and had a problem with cutting on herself.

As much as I am a goal-directed person and try to make things happen, there was no way that I could have orchestrated all of this myself. God must have done it. This experience greatly reinforced my faith that there is a Higher Power, for sure.

If you make the *commitment,* God works out the details. Countless people, including alcoholics and addicts on the spiritual road to recovery, have found this to be true.

Many alcoholics and addicts have a profound and dramatic spiritual awakening experience when they hit bottom, at the moment when they decide to surrender and admit that their addiction has finally defeated them. Others may have a dramatic awakening experience later on in their recovery, at a time when they least expect it. Some, such as many newcomers in Twelve Step programs, may even subconsciously or consciously wait for, anticipate, and hope for something profound and dramatic to happen to them. They may have heard or read about wonderful stories of experiences that other people have had.

For most people in recovery, spiritual awakening develops slowly over time. As described in the Alcoholics Anonymous Big Book, the psychologist William James calls this the "educational variety." It is a learning process, which requires time and continual effort, much like getting a college degree. However, one never graduates or is completely done with the process of spiritual growth. There is always more to learn.

Many have had their experience of spiritual awakening in seemingly unlikely, unglamorous places. There are numerous stories of alcoholic and addicted prisoners in jail cells, addicts on the floors of hospitals and detoxification centers going through withdrawal, and people who come to a moment of realization after a horrible car accident caused by drunk driving. Spiritual awakening can happen at any time and at any place, not only in religious buildings or in pleasant surroundings. For some, it may.

Some people have described their spiritual awakening as an unexplainable feeling of warmth or as a positive force of energy that came into the room and enveloped them in their moment of need. Some have described this as having a strong sense of a powerful and benevolent force. Some say that they actually felt the presence of God. Some describe a glimmer of light. Others describe an internal voice, not of themselves and not in so many words, but on a feeling level, that seems to speak: "You are being taken care of. Everything is going to be all right." They suddenly feel a sense of calm and of deep internal peace.

Many people who had previously been atheists, agnostics, or skeptics have had an entirely unexpected moment of spiritual realization of a Higher Power. Some have come to believe that there must be some kind of a God who took care of them when they hit rock bottom with their addiction, for example, at the moment when they woke up or came to and found that they survived.

People experience spiritual awakening in quite a variety of ways, because this is something of a very personal, individual nature. No one can perform the act of eating food and digesting it for another person; no one can exercise and get in shape for another person; no one can think with another person's mind. Likewise, awakening on a spiritual level is something that can only be accomplished on one's own.

However, other people can be instrumental in providing direction and guidance. Many learn by example, by observing people who have what they want on a spiritual level. This frequently happens when one feels that there is something about a specific person or person whom they can relate to ("If she did it, then maybe I can do it too").

Others choose as examples people whom they do not feel like they have a whole lot in common with, whom they feel they can never be quite like, but who are positive role models or "the ultimate to aspire to." A chosen spiritual role model may be, for example, someone who is world famous like Mother Teresa, Mahatma Gandhi, or Martin Luther King Jr. Some may choose a religious clergy from their church, synagogue, or temple. For some, it may be a more common person, such as the guy next door whom they see as an example of someone who lives a good, spiritually based life because he treats everyone with kindness, has peace of mind, and is genuinely happy.

The Twelve Step literature mentions that people must not, however, put all of their faith in, idolize, or make false gods of other members of the program—that "all AA members have clay feet." An alcoholic or addict can relapse at any time. *All* human beings, not only alcoholics and addicts who are well on the road to recovery, are fallible. No human being is all-powerful or perfect, no matter how far he or she has progressed along spiritual lines.

Personal Stories and Examples: Addressing the Spiritual Void

Marsha, a professional woman in her early thirties, had been suffering with anorexia, bulimia, and self-destructive behavior since her teenage years. Her favorite method of self-injury was taking hot, scalding showers, to the point where her skin would turn bright red and burn. Sometimes, especially when already weak from not eating for several days, she would pass out. Marsha frequently talks about how she successfully recovered from her eating disorders and other self-destructive behaviors once she became involved in and devoted to the practice of Buddhism.

Marsha did not choose to attend any type of formal

recovery program. However, she believed very strongly that her religion "works." After many years of counseling and therapy, and conventional as well as homeopathic medical treatment—which she says have all been of some help—she firmly asserts that the one thing that made the significant difference for her was religion.

Marsha has been maintaining her recovery (as well as being faithful to her religious practice) over the last eight years at the time of this writing. She is no longer ruled by her illness, or the inevitable depression that used to come along with it, and is now a much happier person. She is healthy and physically fit, no longer withdrawn, and no longer looks like she weighs only forty-two pounds.

Some people may elect not to belong to an organized religion, or not to attend a church, temple, or synagogue, or not to attend spiritually focused recovery programs. Many of these people also recover successfully from alcohol and other addictions through other methods of treatment. Many also progress along spiritual lines.

Donald, a recovering alcoholic and cocaine addict from the projects in Compton, California, says that all he has to do is go out into nature and look around in order for him to believe that there is "Something" greater and more powerful than himself. He enjoys getting away from the concrete and brick buildings of the inner city when he can and frequently gets in his Jeep and takes short weekend trips to the woods and to the mountains. Donald once stated, "There must be some kind of God or Higher Power, because I can't make a tree!"

Because I happen to come from a traditional East Coast Catholic background, having been raised primarily by my grandparents, who gave me a very strong spiritual and moral foundation to start out with, I was fortunate enough to be able to address the spiritual concepts early on in recovery. However, it did not all happen for me right away, and it was a struggle.

The hardest part, for me, was developing a more genuine, internal sense of spiritual *awareness*. A lot of my old ideas, especially those about God as a fear-provoking and punishing figure, had to change. A lot of what I learned in Catholic school was very good and is still useful to me to this day, as a core belief system and in terms of "prescriptions for living." But certain things definitely had to be rethought.

Over the years, I had somehow put God on the back burner, eventually becoming ever too busy with college, term papers, work, and the agony of doing a doctoral dissertation and a postdoctoral fellowship. I always said that "someday I wish I could get back into God again, like my grandmother was, when I have enough time." However, I never did have more time, because academic, clinical, and research work is never ending, especially the higher up you go. Fortunately, I somehow found God through default, via my recovery from my addiction to self-injury.

Understanding and addressing addictions from an intellectual perspective was helpful but somehow not enough. As many scientific and academic types often do, I had a very hard time integrating intellectual and spiritual concepts and reasoning, and could not see the connection at the time. One of my former college professors told me to "think of it as being on two different planes—all the academic stuff is on an intellectual plane, and God is on an emotional plane—and you can have both at the same time." This made sense to me. I decided that I had to slow down, had to focus, and that I had to *make* time and room in my life for God, if I wanted to survive. Nothing else was working.

The Twelve Step programs worked very well for me. This has been useful not only in terms of attaining and maintaining abstinence from my addiction, but also in terms of learning how to develop an authentic sense of spirituality and how to most effectively progress along spiritual lines. Although I wish that I did not have to go through the pain and struggle with my addiction to ultimately find God again, I am ever grateful that I now have a very strong and genuine spiritual life and that this is the most important thing in my life.

Going to Twelve Step meetings eventually became something I wanted to do, instead of feeling that it was something I had to do. I came to enjoy them very much. From the very beginning of my recovery, my favorite meetings have always been the ones that are spiritually focused and positive. Now, I also attend church because I want to, not because my second-grade nun said so.

Applications of Twelve Steps to Self-Injury

Because people can become addicted to self-injury just as they can become addicted to alcohol and drugs, Twelve Step programs can be very helpful, as they have been for alcoholics and drug addicts for many years. Many if not most self-injurers have cross-addictions as well, and the risk of addiction substitution is always there.

Over the last several years, Twelve Step meetings specifically for self-injurers have been few and far between, and sometimes nonexistent. Oftentimes, these groups have been of negative focus; that is, on the dynamics of self-injuring as opposed to on recovery. However, there are a lot of other Twelve Step meetings to choose from. (See chapter 8 for lists and descriptions.) Self-injurers who have other co-occurring addictions or who come from alcoholic families may feel most comfortable attending meetings where these issues are addressed. And anyone can attend "open" meetings, even if they do not identify with a particular addiction.

Twelve Step meetings can be a "safe place" for the self-injurer to go, something that is there and available on a regular basis. Being around other people helps a lot—self-injury is not a "party thing"; it is usually done alone in total isolation. Even sitting quietly in the back of the room where a meeting is going on and saying nothing greatly reduces the risk of danger of having another incident. It can also have a very calming effect.

Some types of meetings are a better fit for a particular person than for others. For example, some people prefer small, sharing group meetings. Others prefer large speaker meetings or a group that is all women or all men or specifically for teenagers. It is often suggested that newcomers try out a number of different meetings, instead of just going to one or two and deciding that it's not for them. Meetings are a great place for the recovering alcoholic, addict, or self-injurer to make new social connections, to meet new friends. A *sponsor* is someone who has acquired some time in sobriety, who has done the work of the program, and who is available to help others. A sponsor can help the newly recovering person to go through and work the Twelve Steps of the program.

The Twelve Steps: Basic Tools of Recovery

The Twelve Steps are a simple, straightforward, and action-oriented program for recovery. They were written more than sixty years ago by the founders of Alcoholics Anonymous.

The Twelve Steps of recovery programs such as Alcoholics Anonymous, Al-Anon, and others stemming from this model are the program's basic tools. Following is a list of the Twelve Steps of Alcoholics Anonymous, as well as a list of the Twelve Steps modified for recovery from self-injury. Steps One through Three are *belief* Steps. Steps Four through Nine are *action* Steps. Steps Ten through Twelve are *maintenance* Steps. In summary, these Steps involve

- realizing that we cannot solve our problems alone
- believing that a Power greater than ourselves ("God" or a "Higher Power") can help us
- making a decision to and becoming willing to surrender to the care of God or a Higher Power
- making an honest list of our faults (which should also include our strengths) and sharing this with another person
- making amends for the harm we have caused, whenever possible
- monitoring our thoughts and actions on an ongoing basis, and being willing to admit and make right any of our wrongdoings as soon as they occur
- continuing to improve our relationship with God or a Higher Power, and praying for knowledge and strength
- carrying a message of hope and sharing the benefits we have received through working these Steps with other people who need the same kind of help (for example, other alcoholics, addicts, or self-injurers)
- applying the principles of the Twelve Steps to *all* aspects of our lives

The Twelve Steps of Alcoholics Anonymous*

1. We admitted we were powerless over alcohol—that our lives had become unmanageable.
2. Came to believe that a Power greater than ourselves could restore us to sanity.

---

* The Twelve Steps of Alcoholics Anonymous are taken from *Alcoholics Anonymous,* 3d ed., published by AA World Services, Inc. (AAWS), New York, N.Y., 59–60. Reprinted with the permission of AAWS. (See editor's note on copyright page.)

3. Made a decision to turn our will and our lives over to the care of God *as we understood Him.*

4. Made a searching and fearless moral inventory of ourselves.

5. Admitted to God, to ourselves, and to another human being the exact nature of our wrongs.

6. Were entirely ready to have God remove all these defects of character.

7. Humbly asked Him to remove our shortcomings.

8. Made a list of all persons we had harmed, and became willing to make amends to them all.

9. Made direct amends to such people wherever possible, except when to do so would injure them or others.

10. Continued to take personal inventory and when we were wrong promptly admitted it.

11. Sought through prayer and meditation to improve our conscious contact with God *as we understood Him,* praying only for knowledge of His will for us and the power to carry that out.

12. Having had a spiritual awakening as the result of these steps, we tried to carry this message to alcoholics, and to practice these principles in all our affairs.

The Twelve Steps, Modified for Recovery from Self-Injury *

1. We admitted we were powerless over self-injury—that our lives had become unmanageable.

2. Came to believe that a Power greater than ourselves could restore us to sanity.

3. Made a decision to turn our will and our lives over to the care of God, *as we understood God.*

---

* Adapted from the Twelve Steps of Alcoholics Anonymous with the permission of Alcoholics Anonymous World Services, Inc. (AAWS). (See editor's note on copyright page.)

4. Made a searching and fearless moral inventory of ourselves.
5. Admitted to God, to ourselves, and to another trusted human being the exact nature of our wrongs.
6. Were entirely ready to have God remove all these defects of character.
7. Humbly asked God to remove our shortcomings.
8. Made a list of all persons we had harmed, *including ourselves,* and became willing to make amends to all.
9. Made direct amends to such people, *including ourselves,* wherever possible, except when to do so would injure those involved or others.
10. Continued to take personal inventory and when we were wrong promptly admitted it.
11. Sought through prayer and meditation to improve our conscious contact with God, *as we understood God,* praying only for knowledge of God's will for us and the power to carry that out.
12. Having had a spiritual awakening as the result of these steps, we tried to carry this message to self-injurers and other addicts, and to practice these principles in all our affairs.

Practical Suggestions for Spiritual Growth

So how does one become more spiritual? There are no quick and easy answers or methods that will work the same way for everyone. Remember, spiritual growth is a lifelong process. If one has the *desire,* he or she is already halfway there. The heart and mind will find a way. Here are a few action-oriented suggestions that have helped other people get started.

- **Talk with other people.** Talk with people whom you admire for their spirituality. Find out what they are doing right. Learn from their experience.
- **Read.** You can read the Bible, the Talmud, the Koran, or other spiritual literature. You can read Twelve Step literature; books at the library or the bookstore; books by or about famous spiritual or inspirational leaders.
- **Go to church, temple, synagogue.** Check it out. Attend a service. This is also a great opportunity to meet and talk with religious clergy as well as neighbors and new friends.
- **Go to Twelve Step meetings.** There are meetings to address addictions, and for the families, friends, and concerned others involved in the lives of those who have addictions.
- **Go to a sharing or support group.** For example, there are prayer groups, Bible studies, and teen and youth groups through various religious institutions. There are other sharing groups—such as therapy or support groups for grief and bereavement, or for improving your relationships—that can help.
- **Help those less fortunate than you.** Help the poor, the sick, the lonely, anyone in need of service. An elder member of AA once stated, "I don't care if somebody has only two days clean and sober—he can still help the guy who has only one day."
- **Prayer.** This includes asking for help and also prayers of gratitude.
- **Meditation.** Prayer is talking to God; meditation is the silent act of listening.
- **Personal growth and development.** Efforts to improve yourself as a human being are spiritual. Becoming a better person can be achieved, for example,

through therapy, education or study in some academic area, taking good care of your physical body, working out, sports, or healthy nutrition, so that you can be the best person that you can possibly be.

- **Learn to explore and appreciate nature.** You can go to the desert, mountains, ocean, woods, or the country; watch the sunset; watch a bird in flight; or appreciate the beauty of a flower.

- **Get in touch with your creative side.** Develop your skills and talents in art, music, writing, etc. Or develop an appreciation of the talents of others, for example, by visiting an art gallery, visiting a museum, or going to a concert. Talk with artists and listen to their inspiration.

- **Attend seminars or conferences.** Some are spiritual, such as structured retreats and workshops; some are educational; and some are for personal growth and development.

- **Visit retreat centers or monastic guest houses.** These are good places to go to for quiet thought and contemplation; they are very peaceful and in beautiful settings, usually in the mountains or in the woods. You can go there on your own or on a group retreat with a Twelve Step or religious group. The books *Sanctuaries: The Complete United States* (Kelly 1996) and *A Guide to Monastic Guest Houses* (Regalbuto 1998) contain listings and descriptions of such places throughout the United States.

- **Listen to music.** Gospel, religious songs of your faith, Gregorian or Tibetan monk chants, patriotic songs, designated religious music radio stations.

- **Writing exercises.** Twelve Step–related writing exercises such as doing your moral inventory; spiritual journaling; self-help and personal growth workbooks you can find in the psychology, recovery, or self-help section of your local bookstore or at an online bookstore.

- **Spiritual reminders.** Knickknacks or pictures; notes or Post-its on your computer or bathroom mirror or school notebook, of something meaningful to you (for example, a verse from Scripture or a word or phrase such as *faith* or *trust God*); or wearing a piece of meaningful religious jewelry such as a cross or a Star of David are good ways to remember to stay focused on your spirituality throughout the day.

Finding spiritual meaning in everyday life, and *applying* it, is genuine and beneficial. Successfully applying spirituality to life is explained through the following story:

A wise, elderly foster mother walked through the parking lot of a foster family services agency that serves abused and neglected children (who had all suffered great catastrophes and had been removed from their parents' homes), which was next door to the agency where I was working years ago. Five or six very young children (all preschool age) were following her, all walking in a straight line, all well-behaved, smiling, and happy. A co-worker commented: "How do you do it? Look, they're all being so good, and they all look so happy! I don't know how you do it!" The woman turned to us and stated definitively and without a moment's hesitation: "Put God first. Be committed. Be consistent." That saying caught on at work with the nurses, caught on at my hometown Twelve Step meetings, and is in a picture frame on my desk at work today. Find something meaningful to you.

CHAPTER EIGHT

If You or Someone You Know Self-Injures

As self-injury progresses, the sufferer is in increasing danger of getting caught up in—and sometimes trapped within—a vicious cycle. This involves emotionally escalating to the point of an emergency, wherein the self-injurer feels that she has lost control and that she is going to hurt herself no matter what; then having another incident such as cutting or burning, again and again. Each incident gets progressively worse in terms of severity, because of the increased tolerance of physical pain that has been built up. Coming down, or "crashing," can also progressively get worse.

It is important to become aware of and to understand how the escalation/de-escalation cycle works. (See explanation and figures 2 and 3 in chapter 2.) The goal is to avoid a state of emergency, as soon as possible, by intervening in positive ways. Recognize the danger signals—and take action immediately.

Caught in the Vicious Cycle

Janice's husband walked in the front door, coming home from work late again. She wondered why he was late—was he having an affair? She glared at him. A heated argument soon broke out between the two, this time about her spending too much money on clothes and makeup. The emotional escalating began.

Seeing herself as "the one who wears the pants in the family," the stronger of the two, Janice began to pick on and insult Jack, her quiet, passive, expertly codependent husband. On some level, she was enjoying verbally beating up on him . . . although for a split second she did notice a look of hurt in his eyes. Feeling a momentary twinge of guilt, Janice then began emotionally beating up on herself, bombarded by thoughts of how she was a horrible, bad person to have been so cruel to the man she loves who has given her so much.

Jack raised his voice at Janice, the temples in his head throbbing with rage. Janice suddenly had a childhood flashback of when she was ten years old, alone in the big dark house, her father coming home and screaming at her when he was drunk. . . . Would he hit her, again? This was something her husband promised her he would never do.

She stormed into the spare bedroom and slammed the door. A picture came crashing off the wall, onto the floor. Janice's thoughts were racing around and around. By this time, she was crying and hyperventilating. She opened the drawer on the nearby nightstand, hoping to find a pen or something to hurt herself with, and her acrylic nail broke off. Janice had spent her last fifteen dollars to get her nails done that afternoon; this was what sparked the fight to begin with. She cried hysterically. Drowning in self-pity, all she could think about was how she only did it to look pretty for him; that she shouldn't have had her nails done at all; that she couldn't even hurt herself with those plastic nails because they don't hurt like the real ones; that she shouldn't have done it; that she does everything wrong. . . . The obsessional thoughts became louder and louder, something to the effect of "Gotta cut, gotta cut, gotta cut; I can't take it any-more," until they finally drowned out everything else in the environment, including Jack.

Janice looked over at a lightbulb. In utter desperation, she smashed it and sliced her arms and face with the bro-ken shards of glass.

She locked herself in that room for hours, then days, and would not come out to spend time with her teenage son or younger daughter, the family dog, or her husband, although they all tried to help. Janice sank into a deep depression. She only came out of the room to compulsively overeat (again) when no one else was home, in an attempt to com-fort herself and to stuff her feelings. She was finally feeling better and calm . . . until she stepped on the scale and found that she had gained more weight. The escalation cycle be-gins again . . .

Janice could have interrupted this vicious cycle several times along the way, ideally in the very beginning. For ex-ample, she could have walked away from the heated argu-ment with her husband right away, or at least when she saw that things were getting out of control. Later on in the cycle, she could have gone to an Overeaters Anonymous meeting with her sister, who understood, instead of isolating herself from others.

There are a number of things that a self-injurer like Janice can do to slow herself down in an emergency. Ideally, Janice would have other caring people around whom she could call and count on. People like her sister can be of great help and lend emotional support, especially in times of cri-sis. Sometimes simply just "being there" for someone is enough. However, if the self-injurer finds herself alone in a time of crisis (such as if it's 3 A.M. and there's no one else in the house), there are a number of things that she can do to help herself.

Different things work better for different people. One self-injurer may find, for example, that prayer works wonderfully for her, while another may not be at all inclined toward prayer. Also, different methods may work better at different times for a particular person. Sometimes it depends on where one is and what resources are available at the moment.

If one method of positive diversion does not work for the self-injurer, it's important to explore other alternatives. Be creative; you may come up with some original ideas too!

Part 1: For the Self-Injurer

Things You Can Do in an Emergency

The whole world does not have to know, or will not want to know, about your problem with self-injury. Some people will not understand, and this could be extremely detrimental and discouraging. Remember, you are going to get better; you are in recovery! Be careful whom you tell. Some people will not know how to deal with the information. It is not wise to put your employment, your place of business, or your reputation at school or in your neighborhood in jeopardy.

Use good judgment and be discreet about the positive diversion techniques, as to when and where these methods are used. Not everyone needs to know about your own personal recovery program. For example, you should not go to work with red marking pen writing all over your arms if you are an elementary school teacher (the kids might get scared and scream!). Sitting in your high school class or going to a basketball game with your hand in an ice bucket would only bring on strange looks, nosy questions, and ridicule from uninformed or insensitive others. Using these techniques is something good that you are doing for *you*. You should not put yourself in a position where you have to worry about having to explain it to other people.

Winona, a seven-year-old girl who was sexually abused and put into the foster care system, is a good example of this. Even after she had been removed from the home of her abusers, Winona continued to have flashbacks and episodes of terror. For a long time, she used to bite her nails down to the cuticles whenever she felt scared or anxious. She would often have thin streams of blood running down her fingers. Sometimes the blood would rub off on her clothes, toys, and schoolbooks and papers. Other children would stare. What had started out as a minor self-destructive behavior had eventually become such a severe and compulsive habit that medical treatment was required for infection. The self-injury eventually diminished, then ceased, with therapy. Later, to comfort herself, she would pile up pillows, blankets, and heavy winter jackets in a corner of her bedroom, between the bed and the wall, and sit there for a while until she calmed down. This was her own idea. Winona's foster mother told her that this was okay at home and only in front of her and the family, who understood, but not at school, on the playground, or when her friends came over to play. Even at her young age, she understood this well and complied. With therapy and a lot of love and attention from her new family, Winona got better. She also outgrew this coping behavior, which served her well for a while.

There are a number of different methods that have successfully worked for self-injurers to help them avoid having harmful incidents. A list of strategies follows. Some of the most popular, useful, and practical ones are listed first. Many of these listed items and others can be found in the clinical and research literature on self-injury. Above all, keep an open mind, and have a positive attitude!

Things You Can Do to De-escalate and Divert an Emergency

1. **Reach out.** Call an understanding friend or someone you can trust.
2. **Find a "Safe Place."** This place is somewhere that you choose, where you absolutely refuse to have a destructive incident. Some people might designate a comfortable chair in their house to sit in, attend a Twelve Step meeting, or go over to their grandmother's house.
3. **Breathe.** Take three slow, deep breaths.
4. **Count.** Slowly count to ten.
5. **Pray.** Pray to your Higher Power for strength.
6. **Turn it over.** Turn your addiction, your will, your life over to the care of your Higher Power.
7. **Meditate.** This can be learned by taking a meditation course or reading a book such as *The Relaxation Response* (1975) by Herbert Benson, M.D.
8. **Ice bucket.** Immersing your hand in a bucket of ice can help—the shock of the cold will provide enough of a "jolt" without causing physical scarring. Holding on to an ice-cold can of soda works too, and it's a lot more convenient.
9. **Cry.** Cry if you want to, if you can.
10. **Feel.** Acknowledge and feel your emotions, any emotions, instead of feeling numb.
11. **Write.** You can write in a journal, on paper, or on the computer. You may choose to write a letter or e-mail to a friend or write scattered words, poetry, or words to a song.
12. **Listen.** Listen to music or just to silence.
13. **Draw.** Draw your feelings, draw anything. Colors are good for emotional expression. Go get a box of crayons and start drawing. It will at least put you in

a better mood. Remember how much fun you had in kindergarten?

14. **Use nonharmful alternatives.** Use non-toxic red marking pens (for example, instead of a razor blade) to write on your arms.

15. **Love your pets.** Spend quality time with your cat, dog, or other pet. They will give you unconditional love, and they don't ask you stupid questions.

16. **Eat something.** Eat something that you like and can get enthusiastic about, such as ice cream or a healthy treat like fresh strawberries. (But remember, stay away from caffeine when emotionally escalated!)

17. **Add comfort.** Put on a soft, warm, comforting shirt or jacket. (Flannel or fleece are warm and snuggly material.)

18. **Help somebody else.** When was the last time you gave a homeless person a quarter? Bring food over to someone who is sick. Visit an elderly person who is alone; read to a blind child; volunteer at a hospital, AIDS hospice, or homeless shelter.

19. **Clean the house.** Vacuum and dust. Clean out your closet and give your old clothes to a charitable organization.

20. **Walk.** Take a walk outside, or around the block. The fresh air and sunshine will help.

21. **Physical exercise.** Sports, working out, walking, running, bike riding, etc. will give you energy, and the endorphin release will do you good.

22. **Go shopping.** Keep in mind that window-shopping can be just as good and less expensive than real shopping.

23. **Exercise your brain.** Do crossword puzzles or solve complex mathematical problems.

24. **Focus.** Do some kind of focused, absorbing visual

type of work or craft—for example, needlepoint, knitting, embroidery, or a jigsaw puzzle.

25. **Read.** Read a good book. Go to a library or bookstore and browse.

26. **Look at pictures.** Look at pictures in some of your favorite magazines.

27. **Watch the news.** Turn on the TV news and see who has it worse than you.

28. **Spend quality time with a child.** Read, play, draw, color—have fun! Children are generally happy and lighthearted and are enjoyable to be around.

29. **Go to a movie, watch a video, or play a computerized TV game.** (But remember, nothing violent or with blood and guts, which can be an emotional trigger.)

30. **Socialize.** Do some type of fun social activity with people you like.

31. **Embrace religion.** Go to a church, temple, or synagogue.

32. **Go out into nature.** Go to the mountains, the beach, or the woods. Look at a sunset, or look up at the stars in the sky at night.

33. **Walk away.** Remove yourself immediately from a negative situation. Walk away from a heated argument. Leave the party if people start using illegal drugs.

34. **Be productive.** Balance your checkbook, finish your homework, etc. The positive reinforcement of accomplishing something will help you feel better.

35. **Make a list.** Make a list such as "Goals for My Future" or "Things to Look Forward To."

36. **Do some writing exercises.** Do the writing exercises in chapter 9; find others in self-help books at the bookstore; think of some ideas of your own.

37. **Drive or ride.** Take a long, peaceful drive, or ride around on the subways, buses, or trains.
38. **Go to an art gallery or museum.** Visual stimuli is very helpful to self-injurers.
39. **Improve your appearance.** Experiment with different looks. Get your hair cut or style it differently. Experiment with clothing and fashion.
40. **Relax.** Take a nap.
41. **Have an "attitude of gratitude."** Even if you don't feel grateful at the moment, start with the basics: for example, "I have a roof over my head; I have food on my table; I have two arms and two legs and can walk and can see." There are many people in the world who don't even have that.
42. **Sing.** Sing out loud. The endorphin release will do you good.
43. **Dance.** Find somewhere with live music or dance in your own living room.
44. **Role-play.** Role-play a situation—with a positive, desired outcome—with a friend.
45. **Cook.** Cook or bake something you like, for yourself or for someone else.
46. **Look at photographs.** Look at photo albums or pictures of happy times you've had (such as birthday parties or fun times with family or friends).
47. **Search the Web.** Search the Internet for a fun topic that captures your interest (for example, a place you might like to travel to sometime, such as the Great Pyramids in Egypt).
48. **Look at your accomplishments.** Look at evidence of your accomplishments (for example, a good grade on a math test or a sports trophy).
49. **Take a shower or bath.** This is a good way to relax and relieve tension.

50. **Say this prayer over and over:** "Thank you God for removing this obsession (for example, with cutting, alcohol, etc.). Believe it. It has worked for many people and can work for you too.

Carrying a Short List

For practical purposes, some people have found it useful to make a short list of diversion techniques to carry around with them or to memorize. Sometimes, it is more frustrating to look through a long list when in a crisis mode. This is because when in the throes of an emotional crisis, problem-solving and decision-making abilities may become impaired. The short list can include five or ten thoughts or actions that have been most helpful to you in the past to successfully avoid having an incident.

Megan, a thirty-six-year-old teacher, graduate student, and mother, made this list of things that help at a time when she was having a very serious problem with relapsing early in her recovery. She referred to it during times of emergency.

Megan's List of Things That Help:

Ice bucket
Getting away from my husband for the moment
Call a friend who knows and understands
Pray
Think about the fact that they could take my children away
   from me if I do this

Patty, a thirteen-year-old girl who was repeatedly sexually abused by her father from the ages of five through twelve, made this list at about a year into her recovery. She had not had an episode of self-injury for a year or any episodes of drinking or using drugs. She was succeeding in her residential group home program and was regularly attending and getting good grades in school for the first time in her life. Patty was also working on her relationship with her mother in multi-family group therapy.

Patty's List of Things That Help:

Going to my Christian youth group at church

Singing in the choir—I get a real high from it

Giving up my "Gothic" look: the black nail polish, the black lipstick and dark makeup, no more homemade tattoos or dressing weird

Spending time with my friends (but not the ones I got into trouble with)

Showing my good grades and awards to my mother and my grandmother

Looking at my modeling pictures

Remembering what Tynisha (another group home resident) told me: "If you cut on yourself, they'll think you're a psychopathic bitch and throw you in a mental hospital. It happened to me when I was twelve."

Be Aware: Things That Agitate/Make It Worse

One of the hallmarks of self-injury especially, and other addictions as well, is that the person is more likely to have an episode or a relapse when agitated or angry. It is helpful to know what these things are for *you*.

Make a list of the things that upset you or are likely to act as triggers. Add to the list as you think of more things over time. Michelle, a longtime self-injurer, put this list together:

Michelle's List of Things That Hurt/Make It Worse:

1. *Being around certain people*
2. *Keep looking at scars*
3. *PMS*
4. *Keep talking about wanting to hurt myself*
5. *Loud noises: especially leaf blowers, shrill music, and fireworks*
6. *Having a cigarette*
7. *Bright, glaring, or unpleasant colors (especially red)*
8. *Hanging on to and harping on anger/resentments (for example, toward people who have hurt me in the past)*
9. *Sexual arousal*
10. *Sexual interactions with anybody when upset*
11. *Being laughed at, made fun of, or when someone rolls their eyes at me*
12. *Getting behind with my housecleaning and chores, to the point where the apartment is a mess*
13. *Getting scolded by my boss when I don't get my work done on time*
14. *Financial fear*

The Main Things Self-Injurers Should *Not* Do

1. Do not *hurt yourself in any way.*
Make the *commitment* that you will not hurt yourself, first to *yourself* and then others. Consider making a promise to God or a Higher Power and/or to another important person in your life. This may be, for example, your mother, spouse, significant other, child, therapist, or sponsor.

2. Do not isolate yourself from other people.
Researchers studying the field of addictions have found that a leading cause of relapse is *isolation*. This is important to remember, especially in times of vulnerability and crisis.

3. Do not give up.
No matter how frustrated and discouraged you may get when emotionally escalated, do not stop trying to help yourself. Keep thinking of the bigger picture. You will not always feel this bad. Tomorrow is a new day. Remember that you do not want to hurt important people in your life and that you do not want to lose your job or get kicked out of school.

Part 2: For Concerned Others

When to Get Help for the Self-Injurer

Ideally, help should be sought and obtained as soon as possible. Depending on the immediacy and seriousness of the situation, this can range from calling 911 in an emergency for a life-threatening physical injury, to making an appointment for therapy in the near future with a mental health professional, or arranging for transportation to a local Twelve Step support group meeting. If not addressed, the problem with self-injury can get worse over time, with potentially catastrophic outcomes and end results.

If you are a parent, friend, or other concerned person in the self-injurer's life, some guidelines as to when to seek help are

1. when the self-injurer is in imminent physical danger (for example, has a physical injury that requires medical attention)
2. when there is visible evidence of a self-inflicted wound or injury

3. when the self-injurer appears to meet or can identify with various items on list 3 in chapter 1: Self-Injury Checklist (pages 29–31)
4. when the self-injurer has obsessive thoughts about hurting herself
5. when the self-injurious behavior becomes compulsive
6. when the problem with self-injury or concurrent emotional states (such as depression and anxiety) interfere with work or school, health, money, and/or interpersonal relationships
7. when the self-injurer asks for help, including hinting about or alluding to a need for help

What Other People Can Do to Help the Self-Injurer

There are many ways in which family and friends can help the struggling self-injurer. One can

- provide encouragement
- provide moral support
- help the self-injurer to find professional help

Obtaining professional help as necessary must be first and foremost, and remain primary. Trained medical, psychiatric, and/or psychological professionals are necessary to address this serious problem. Concerned others in the self-injurer's life cannot take their place.

However, parents, family members, and spouses or significant others can help tremendously by participating in the self-injurer's therapy. Although it may sometimes be emotionally difficult for them as well, they can attend and make a commitment to be consistent with family or couples counseling.

A friend or concerned other can accompany the self-injurer to a medical facility or counseling session to provide moral support. Offering a ride or even just going along with

202 A Plan for Recovery

the person in need and sitting in the waiting room can be helpful. These are ways to make a difference.

"Being there" in times of crisis or when the person who has a problem with self-injury wants to talk (either on the phone or in person) can help. Any self-injurer will tell you that there are times when she does not want to or is afraid to be alone.

It is also important for concerned others to understand the self-injurer's individual needs and preferences. Helpers should not impose their own ideas, which although kindly thought out and well intentioned, may be the entirely wrong thing to do. Remember, when the self-injurer is in a state of intense escalation and pending emergency, she is extremely vulnerable. She may become defensive or may even lash out if she feels threatened or if she feels that someone is trying to take away her sense of control.

Whom You Can Approach for Help

There are many people who can be approached to provide help and assistance for the struggling self-injurer. As mentioned previously, medical, psychiatric, and/or psychological professionals should be consulted as necessary. The conclusion of this chapter lists resources of where to find help.

Religious clergy from churches, temples, or synagogues are good people to consult with. These people will likely be familiar with community resources and can also provide moral support, spiritual help, and guidance to the self-injurer and the concerned parent, friend, or family member. Prayer can be very powerful too. Sometimes a conversation with or a visit from someone such as a priest, rabbi, or minister can help influence the self-injurer to make the commitment to stop hurting herself and to get help.

Many teenagers have come across the problem of self-injury in friends, siblings, and peers. If you are someone in this age group, realize that the teenage self-injurer will most likely forbid you to tell her parents or guardians about this problem. She may even threaten to end the friendship if you do. In order to be a *real* friend, you must be accountable and act in her best interest. Tell an adult who is in charge.

The problem of self-injury is most prevalent among teenagers—and is becoming a rapidly growing and widespread problem. It is therefore important that those who work with children and teenagers, especially school personnel, become aware of what self-injury is and how they can best be of help to those whom they serve.

Within elementary, junior high, and high school settings, one can approach school nurses, school psychologists, and school counselors for help. However, the degree of help needed by self-injurers is generally beyond the scope of what these professionals can provide at school. But they can help to facilitate referral to other resources in the community. Because the child or teenager who has a problem with self-injury spends most of her time at school, it is good for her to have someone there who knows and understands, who can act as a liaison between the school and the outside therapist, and who can provide help and support, especially in times of crisis.

Teachers, principals, and school administrators should be aware of the dynamics of self-injury as well. An incident can happen right there in the classroom, and the teacher should know what to do. For example, a student can hurt herself with a readily available, everyday device such as a paper clip or pencil, or even with her own fingernails. She can do this either quietly or while making a scene. This may include crying out, screaming, knocking over desks and chairs, and hitting and kicking people who get in her way. School principals and assistant principals can lend the voice of authority by strongly encouraging the self-injuring child and her family to get professional help. They can effectively intervene with the parent or guardian, the child, and the teacher.

Where to Go for Help

There are many places to go for help if self-injury and/or other addictions become a problem. Look for options that are most appropriate to your situation. At the time of this writing, there are not a whole lot of choices available that are self-injury specific. But don't despair. A list of resources that can be explored is included below.

In order to find these resources within your local area, you can start by calling directory assistance or by searching both the white and the yellow pages of the phone book. You can also search the Internet.

Check with your local community hospitals, treatment centers, mental health centers, and social service agencies. You may also want to check with local churches and other places of worship. The people on the other end of the line may have information that can be useful to you, and they can at least help give you a sense of direction.

Word of mouth is another good option. You can talk to others in similar situations or to people who may have information about available resources. For example, parents who are looking for a private therapist to work with their teenage son or daughter can talk to other parents and teachers and personnel at their child's school. Parents can ask about recommendations for therapists in the local community who specialize in and work well with adolescents.

Resource Guide

I. Medical Help
   Hospital emergency rooms
   Hospital or community urgent care centers

II. Psychological/Psychiatric Help and Counseling

Community mental health centers (many take low-income clients)

Department of Mental Health

Psychiatric inpatient hospitals and hospital units

Psychiatric/psychological outpatient treatment centers

Psychological trauma treatment centers

Inpatient recovery programs: for alcohol; addictions; eating disorders; self-injury

Residential treatment centers for children and adolescents

College and university student counseling centers

Within elementary, junior high, and high schools: school nurses, school psychologists, school counselors

Private therapists: psychiatrists, psychologists, psychiatric nurses, social workers, licensed counselors/therapists

III. Twelve Step Programs: Alcoholism and Addictions

Note: There are many types of groups available within some of the larger groups. For example, there are groups for women only and groups for men only; groups for gays and lesbians; groups for teenagers; groups that offer child care or handicap access; groups in languages other than English. Some groups have or include a specific focus—for example, there are Overeaters Anonymous meetings with focus on anorexia nervosa and bulimia. Look at the program directory listings, or ask around.

Alcoholics Anonymous

Narcotics Anonymous

Cocaine Anonymous

Drugs Anonymous

Marijuana Anonymous

Smokers Anonymous
Overeaters Anonymous
Debtors Anonymous
Gamblers Anonymous
Workaholics Anonymous
Sex Addicts Anonymous
Sexaholics Anonymous
Sex and Love Addicts Anonymous

IV. Twelve Step Programs: For Family and Friends of
Alcoholics and Addicts

Al-Anon: A Twelve Step program for family and friends
of alcoholics. Founded by Lois, the wife of Bill W., the
cofounder of Alcoholics Anonymous.

Alateen: A Twelve Step program for teenagers who have
family or friends that are alcoholics. It is run by
teenagers and guided by members of Al-Anon.

Nar-Anon: A Twelve Step program, similar to Al-Anon,
for people who are dealing with narcotic addiction in
a family member or friend.

Adult Children of Alcoholics (ACA): A Twelve Step program for adults whose parents were or are alcoholics.

Families Anonymous: A Twelve Step program for parents and grandparents who are concerned about
the use of mind-altering substances or related behavioral problems in their children (including their adult
children).

Co-Dependents Anonymous (CoDa): A Twelve Step program for people who want to overcome their issues
with unhealthy, interdependent, addictive relationships. Members have a desire for healthy, functional
relationships with themselves as well as with others.

V. Other Twelve Step Programs

Emotions Anonymous (EA): A Twelve Step program to help people recover from a variety of emotional difficulties, including severe chronic mental illness, depression, anxiety, and phobias. Many members have dual diagnosis of clinical emotional disturbance and alcohol or drug addiction.

Parents Anonymous: A Twelve Step program to help parents effectively deal with issues of child raising and appropriate discipline.

Incest Survivors Anonymous: A Twelve Step program that deals with all types of childhood sexual abuse, including ritualistic abuse. Members have a desire to come to see themselves as "survivors" instead of "victims."

Survivors of Incest Anonymous: A Twelve Step program for people who have been sexually abused by a family member or other trusted adult.

VI. Where to Search for Reading Materials

1. Local bookstores, especially the major chains. Look in the "Psychology" or "Self-Help" sections.

2. College and university libraries: textbooks and academic journal articles in the fields of psychology, medicine, nursing, and social work. Libraries at university medical schools have the biggest and best selections.

3. Twelve Step meetings: literature, books, and pamphlets on alcoholism and other addictions. Some are free and others are available at a nominal cost, usually on a table in the back of the room. Or, you can ask the meeting secretary or literature representative.

4. Mail-order book catalogs: from psychological, medical, or addictions and recovery organizations.
5. Internet bookstores.
6. Internet: search for relevant topics and Web sites.

CHAPTER NINE

Writing Tools for Recovery

Following are a number of writing exercises for the self-injurer who wants to recover. There is no one right way of completing the assignments; the key is to make this personal and meaningful to *you*. This can be a fun experience, if you make it that way. Some may want to share their thoughts and ideas with a trusted friend, therapist, or spiritual director—with someone who will listen, not censure or judge.

Write from the heart and from the mind. Be honest. You will have a much better chance of recovery if you make the time and effort to put some quality work into it. The act of writing things down on paper makes them more "real," instead of fleeting thoughts and images. Once you write something down, it is more likely that you will remember it and that you will actually do what you said you were going to do. It is also greatly reinforcing to take your writings out a year (or however long) later and see how much *progress* you've made. You will get out of it what you put into it.

The No Self-Destruction Contract, Problem Behaviors and Substances Log, Impulse Manager, and Relapse/Setback Manager are tools that can and should be used in therapy. Samples are included for illustrative purposes, but feel free to improvise. Come up with your own good ideas also, and make this meaningful and something that will work for you.

I. Survival Tools: To Use in Therapy
    1. No Self-Destruction Contract
    2. Problem Behaviors and Substances Log
    3. Impulse Manager
    4. Relapse/Setback Manager

II. Independent Writing Exercises for the Recovering Self-Injurer
    1. Negative Beliefs and Positive Alternatives
    2. Gratitude
    3. Journaling/Life Writings
    4. Reasons to Get Better
    5. My Goals and Aspirations
    6. Controlling My Anger
    7. How Self-Injury Has Harmed Me
    8. My Ideal Day
    9. Things I Like to Do and Things to Look Forward To

I. Survival Tools: To Use in Therapy

1. No Self-Destruction Contract

The No Self-Destruction Contract is a valuable tool to be used in therapy, whether in an outpatient, hospital, or residential treatment setting. The purpose is for the self-injurer to take an active role in making an *agreement* with her therapist and/or other primary treatment staff member(s) and to put it in writing. It is a formal contract, which will be signed, dated, and witnessed.

    Violating the contract means breaking a commitment

and breaking a promise. In some instances, there may be definitive rules and consequences set by the primary therapist or by treatment center policy, such as termination from the hospital or residential program if one self-injures or uses alcohol or drugs.

Quite important, the contract needs to be *relevant to* and *fully understood by* the particular self-injurer for whom it is intended. For instance, with adolescents, the wording must be straightforward and simple enough for the teen to understand. What is highly effective clinically is for the person in treatment—especially teenagers because they usually have a language (slang words, hip sayings, etc.) of their own—to come up with her own words and ideas, with the assistance of the therapist. However, most kids usually don't like to do the actual pen-and-paper writing part, and if asked, this will likely bring up resistance. It is best for the clinician to offer to do so, right in the beginning.

In order to be personally relevant, with respect to culture, as well as clearly understood, the contract must be written in the self-injurer's primary language (Spanish, Chinese, etc.). One must consider the many people, especially in large cities such as Los Angeles and New York, for whom English is a second language. The use of a qualified translator should be enlisted if necessary.

The No Self-Destruction Contract is *for* the self-injurer, and it is *about* her.

Following are some guidelines regarding important points to be included, some suggested wording, and a sample contract.

1. The self-injurer must *commit to* stop all methods of deliberate self-harm (for example, cutting, burning, hitting herself, etc.)
2. If the self-injurer has other concurrent self-destructive

addictive behaviors of concern, such as problems with alcohol, illegal or legal drugs, or bulimia, she must make the commitment to stop. Addiction substitution should be clearly understood and prevented.

3. In times of danger of self-injury, and particularly if suicidal ideation is present, the self-injurer should remove, or have someone else remove, all dangerous/lethal items from her immediate environment.

4. The self-injurer needs to commit to treatment. This may include not AWOL'ing from a hospital or residential treatment program and following the rules and clinical recommendations; committing to attending outpatient therapy sessions on a regular basis; regularly attending Twelve Step program meetings such as Alcoholics Anonymous or Narcotics Anonymous, as agreed on by the self-injurer and her therapist/primary treatment staff.

5. If having suicidal thoughts, the self-injurer will immediately call a twenty-four-hour crisis hotline and/or the therapist's emergency number, as agreed on by her and her therapist. The phone numbers should be written into the contract and therefore readily available. If in a hospital or residential treatment center, the self-injurer will immediately seek help from an appropriate staff member within the facility.

6. If there are consequences to and stipulations regarding breaking the contract, such as being dismissed from a hospital or treatment program, or for missing therapy sessions, this must be spelled out, made clear, and understood.

7. Positive alternative action plans for when one is feeling the urge to self-destruct should be written into the contract. The self-injurer is to commit to trying these.

8. It is helpful for the self-injurer to come up with a few main, very important reasons for her *not* to engage in self-destructive behaviors and write these into the contract (for example, "The county may take my children away from me" or "I'll have scars forever and will regret it").

Sample No Self-Destruction Contract
(for a seventeen-year-old girl in outpatient therapy, written with her therapist in family session with her mother)

I, Suzie S, now make the commitment to stop all self-injury and other stuff that hurts me. This means that I will not hurt myself by cutting, burning, hitting, scratching with fingernails, or anything else at all, whatsoever. It also means that I will not drink alcohol or use drugs, no matter what my friends say. If I am in a place where people are using illegal drugs, like at a friend's house, I will leave, for sure.

I promise to get rid of all the stuff kept hidden in my room to hurt myself, like mostly razor blades. I will not get any more. I will not bring alcohol or drugs into the house. I also understand that since I'm a minor, my mother can search my room whenever she wants to and that she is doing this because she wants to help me.

I agree to attend all my therapy sessions like I'm supposed to. I can be trusted to take the bus to get there and back after school. I will go to the AA meeting on Monday nights with my sister and her husband.

There are important reasons why I should never hurt myself. For me, these are

1. *I might get kicked out of my high school.*
2. *I might get kicked off my volleyball team and not get a college scholarship.*

3. *It would hurt my mom really bad.*

If I feel like hurting myself, I know that there are many other things I can try first that have helped other people like me. I agree to do at least one or more of these things that I have chosen:

1. *call a friend*
2. *pray*
3. *write in my journal*

I am not suicidal, but if I ever were, I agree to call a twenty-four-hour crisis hotline. If I am in serious danger of harming myself or if I am feeling out of control, I will call one or both of the following:

Dr. Jones (xxx) xxx-xxxx
Therapist's emergency number

(xxx) xxx-xxxx
Twenty-four-hour crisis hotline

_____
Suzie S.   *Date*

Witness: _____
Anna S. (Mother)   *Date*

_____
Dr. Jones (Therapist)   *Date*

2. Problem Behaviors and Substances Log

The Problem Behaviors and Substances Log is a tool that will help the self-injurer to track the frequency and severity of her self-destructive behaviors, including self-injury and alcohol and drug use. Over a time period of thirty days she will be able to see patterns, target areas of concern, and track her rate of improvement. Logs can be reviewed at various designated time periods, starting from the beginning of the recovery process and/or therapeutic treatment. For example, one's rate of progress can be reviewed at thirty days, sixty days, ninety days, six months, and one year. This tool will help the self-injurer to be truly *accountable*. A sample log can be found on page 216, and a blank log is on page 217.

3. Impulse Manager

The Impulse Manager is a simple behavioral log that will help the self-injurer to control and understand her impulses to self-injure. It can also be used for alcohol and drug abuse and other self-destructive behaviors. Those with multiple addictions in addition to self-injury should be sure to include these! This tool addresses the cognitive (factual/situational), the negative thought processes, and the emotional (feeling) components of wanting to act out behaviorally. The goal is to come up with ideas for *positive action* as soon as possible, when one is feeling emotionally escalated and has the urge to self-destruct. A sample Impulse Manager tool is on page 218, and a blank log is on page 219.

4. Relapse/Setback Manager

The Relapse/Setback Manager is a simple tool that will help the struggling self-injurer to track and understand what happened to bring on a relapse and why she acted out. The focus is on acknowledging feelings, seeing both the long-term and short-term consequences, coming up with positive alternatives, and developing strategies for what to do immediately to get back on track and on the road to recovery. A sample Relapse/Setback Manager can be found on page 220, and a blank log is on page 221.

Sample Problem Behaviors and Substances Log

Date: _June 24 '01_

In the last thirty days

Problem behaviors and substances	Severity level 1 = low to 10 = high	Number of days I used	Number of times I was high or out of control	Number of times I successfully avoided urge to use	Comments
Self-injury	9	11 or 12	11 or 12	1	This is serious—I need to get help
Alcohol	3	4 or 5	3		Weekends only—parties and out with friends
Amphetamines					
Barbiturates					
Cocaine					
Designer drugs					
Inhalants					
Hallucinogens					
Heroin/opiates					
Marijuana					
Pills: over-the-counter					
Pills: prescription					
Anorexia					
Bulimia	5	3 or 4			Can't keep my weight down
Compulsive overeating					
Other: shoplifted	1	1		2	Shoplifted lipstick at drugstore

Problem Behaviors and Substances Log

In the last thirty days

Date: _____

Problem behaviors and substances	Severity level 1 = low to 10 = high	Number of days I used	Number of times I was high or out of control	Number of times I successfully avoided urge to use	Comments
Self-injury					
Alcohol					
Amphetamines					
Barbiturates					
Cocaine					
Designer drugs					
Inhalants					
Hallucinogens					
Heroin/opiates					
Marijuana					
Pills: over-the-counter					
Pills: prescription					
Anorexia					
Bulimia					
Compulsive overeating					
Other:					

Sample Impulse Manager

_, time, location	I see and hear	I think	I feel	Positive actions taken	Results and comments
Saturday, 6/9/01 5:00 P.M. At home, in kitchen	Roommate spilled coffee on my term paper	Did she do it on purpose? Wish she'd leave. I was stupid for leaving my stuff there.	Angry Resentful Mad at her Mad at myself	Went to other room to chill out Called my sister and calmed down Reprinted my term paper from my computer	Calmed down and did not self-injure
Sunday, 6/24/01 6:30 P.M. At parents' house	Dad's drunk again He yelled at Mom and threw dinner plate on floor	He'll never stop	Scared Sad Hopeless		Burned hole in my hand with cigarette Should have called somebody

Impulse Manager

Date, time, location	I see and hear	I think	I feel	Positive actions taken	Results and comments

Sample Relapse Manager
What Happened, Why, and Getting Back on Track

Date, time, location	Triggering situation	Feelings	Negative behavior(s)	Consequences (short-term)		Positive alternatives	What I'm going to do now to recover
Saturday. 6/23/01 3:00 P.M. The mall	Saw my boyfriend at the mall. making out with another girl	Anger Rage Jealousy	Left my friends there and walked home, got high (coke). slashed arm with knife, stole bottle of Dad's whiskey from cabinet and drank some	Painful cut on my arm Got blood on my new shirt Threw up from the whiskey		Pray Call a friend Cry Call crisis hot-line	Call my sponsor right away Tell my therapist the whole truth Get to some meetings and meet new people Break up with my boyfriend
				Consequences (long-term)			
				The cut will probably leave an ugly scar			

Relapse Manager

What Happened, Why, and Getting Back on Track

Date, time, location	Triggering situation	Feelings	Negative behavior(s)	Consequences (short-term)	Positive alternatives	What I'm going to do now to recover
				Consequences (long-term)		

II. Independent Writing Exercises for the Recovering Self-Injurer

1. Negative Beliefs and Positive Alternatives

Negative beliefs and attitudes are self-destructive in and of themselves. They may come to us from our parents, our religion, our culture, influential others from childhood such as teachers, or from jealous peers and so-called friends. Particularly if one has been abused as a child (physically, sexually, or emotionally/verbally), these negative beliefs can become internalized. The fact is, none of these core negatives need be true. The key to recovery is to make a conscious effort to change; to come up with positive alternative beliefs and attitudes.

There is such a thing as a self-fulfilled prophecy; that is, what one believes can come to materialize. For example, if one has the core belief that "No one will ever love me," one may present herself in a negative way to others, and thus push people away.

Even if you can't see the positive right now, think in terms of, What would I like to be? How *can* I be?

Following is an example of what Stephanie, a young adult struggling with the beginning stages of recovery, put on her list. At the time, she was getting over (yet another) bad relationship, had put on a few extra pounds, and was stressed about dealing with her five-year-old hyperactive son, who was always getting into trouble and breaking things. Stephanie was effectively working on changing her negative attitude and building her overall self-esteem and self-confidence in therapy.

Negative Beliefs	Positive Alternative Beliefs
I'm not smart.	I have my diploma and am good at my job.
I'm not attractive.	People tell me I'm pretty. I could do more to improve my looks.
No one will ever love me.	My mother loves me, my kids love me, and God loves me. I'll meet the right man someday.
I can't stop drinking/drugging/using.	I can be clean and sober, if I really want to.
I can't control my temper.	I can control my temper, if I count to ten.
It's too late for me.	It's never too late. Mrs. Smith got sober and went back to get her college degree when she was fifty-two.

2. Gratitude

It is important to remember to have and maintain an "attitude of gratitude." No matter how bad things may seem, they could always be worse. If you have your life, you have a lot to be thankful for. If you compare yourself to everyone else around you, sure, you can always find someone else who seems to have it better than you do. Most of us tend to buy into the "greener grass" syndrome: the grass is always greener on the other side. For example, one may think, "I wish I had her good fortune, good looks, rich parents, or perfect boyfriend, instead of what I have." Accepting the things that you cannot change and making positive changes where you can are the key.

Start by making a list of ten things to be grateful for and repeat it every night before you go to sleep. You can also keep adding to the list, to see how many things you can come up with. If so inclined, you may offer it as a prayer of thankfulness to God or your Higher Power. This exercise will change your frame of mind, especially if practiced regularly.

In the very beginning of my recovery, it was hard for me to think of even two or three things to be grateful for. Within a very short time, and with continued recovery, the lists expanded exponentially. My first lists were pretty basic, but functional. (See example below.)

One word of caution: Don't say or even think "yeah, but . . ." after any of the items on your list. That would defeat the purpose!

Things to Be Grateful For

I have food in my refrigerator
I have a roof over my head
my cat
my sobriety
good friends
good job
am in good health
lunch was good
I now have hope
I didn't relapse today

---

3. Journaling/Life Writings

Many people find it useful to keep a journal or a personal diary to write about their thoughts, feelings, ideas, and events that happened. Do what works for you—some people like to write every day, once a week, or only when they want to. If it becomes a required, nagging obligation that you do not want to deal with, or merely a way to self-criticize on paper, it will not be productive. Use whatever format you want to—words, phrases, poetry, drawings, etc. Make it an enjoyable experience, something that you look forward to doing. Sharing this with a therapist, if so desired, can be greatly beneficial also.

As a clinician, I have had much more success in asking teenage girls to write in their journals only when they felt like it, not every day, and emphasizing that they did not "have to." This was for them and about them, and nobody else. They did not have to show me what they wrote about, but if they wanted to, I would be very much interested and would listen to what they had to say. They usually did, without my even having to ask during the next therapy session. They could write slang or bad words if they wanted to, and were told not to worry about spelling, punctuation, grammar, or whether it looks neat or sloppy. They could draw pictures if they wanted to or write short stories, poetry, or whatever came to mind.

A seventeen-year-old boy on my counseling caseload in a nonpublic school asked me, "What if I wrote a rap song? Would you want to read it?" He ended up writing numerous rap songs over the course of the school year and enthusiastically shared them with me as well as with his most trusted teachers. Edwin's songs were quite good and expressive of his deepest thoughts, fears, and feelings that he otherwise could not share with anyone. Much of it was about his father, who recently died of a gunshot wound, and whom he missed very much. His mother was depressed and preoccupied, and could not "be there" for him. Edwin made significant progress in therapy and graduated from high school successfully.

4. Reasons to Get Better

Sometimes staying in the problem (of self-injury, or alcohol or drug addiction, or even a physical illness) serves a purpose, albeit on a subconscious level. However, such purposes are negative and further destructive to one's life and character. Not to mention, this is utterly shattering to one's self-esteem.

For example, having an affliction can be used as a viable excuse to not take responsibility for oneself (for example, financially, by not being able to work and relying on parents' resources long after it is appropriate) or to not take responsibility for one's actions (for example, "I didn't know what I was doing, I was drunk!"). Staying in the problem may also function as a way to get sympathy, help, or caretaking from other people in nonhealthy ways.

The alternative is to come up with reasons to get better. This needs to be brought to the forefront of consciousness, remembered, and reinforced. Keep adding to the list as time goes on, as you think of new things.

Here is an example of what Sherry, a single mother in early recovery from a multitude of addictions, put on her list. At the time, she was on a leave of absence from her job for stress-related depression.

Reasons to Get Better

1. *Be there for my daughter*
2. *Get back to work*
3. *Have some savings in case of an emergency and for my daughter's college*
4. *Am losing my friends*
5. *Am dependent on state disability, which makes me more depressed*

---

5. My Goals and Aspirations

Writing about goals and aspirations for your future is an extremely beneficial exercise. It is also a lot of fun. This will keep you focused on moving forward, always toward bigger and better things. Reviewing these writings months or even years later can be a great positive reinforcement, especially if you accomplish even some of the things you set out to do.

One very effective exercise is to set goals for designated time periods. For example, one may want to start with "Just for Today," and move on to three months, six months, one year, five years, and ten years from now.

Following are some examples of areas that you may want to cover:

1. About my recovery (from self-injury, alcohol or drugs, etc.)
2. Health; physical fitness; well-being
3. Emotional (for example, control my anger)
4. Work or school
5. Family
6. Friendships; social life
7. Love; dating; romantic relationships; marriage
8. Spiritual
9. Finances (start a savings account and watch it grow, etc.)
10. Things I want to do for fun (for example, travel, take up a sport)
11. My daily routine (for example, get up earlier, keep the house clean)

In my experience in working with both teenagers and adults in therapy, I have found that a good way of doing this writing exercise is to tell the client to "start at the top and work your way down toward reality." This works well especially for people who are not motivated or who have a tough time getting started.

Rosa, a seventeen-year-old girl in residential placement who was struggling with severe alcohol and drug addiction (including heroin) among other things, had a hard time getting started. At that time she was not showing much motivation or enthusiasm about anything. However, because of being exceptionally bright and having a lot of God-given potential, she still managed to slide by and do well in school with minimal effort. Working on this list together in a counseling session, with her houseparent present, I told her: "I would not ask you kids to do anything that is too hard or that I wouldn't be willing to do myself. If you promise not to laugh (of course knowing we all would and that it would lighten up the atmosphere and get her motivated), I'll tell you something I put on my list: I fly over all the traffic, in my own personal helicopter, and land on the rooftop of this agency to come to work. So don't be afraid to sound too grandiose or unrealistic; have some fun with this." What she came up with on her own, after stating several times, "No, that's not realistic," was that she would graduate as valedictorian from her high school in one and a half years. She did.

Rosa also met or at least made significant progress toward her smaller, more easily attainable goals along the way. We set her goals for three months, six months, one year, and into the future. We reviewed the goals several times along the way, sometimes revising, adding to, or checking off things that she accomplished. Rosa's goals included the following: Get good grades; Don't AWOL from the group home; Don't use drugs; Get a part-time job; Open a savings account; Use better judgment about boys.

Another strategy for doing this exercise is to make a list (for example, write down four or five goals or resolutions that you want to accomplish for the New Year), and send it or e-mail it to a friend. Have the friend send his or her list to you. Putting it in writing, and sharing it with another person, makes it more real, keeps you accountable, and will put you in the right frame of mind to actually do what you set out to do.

6. Controlling My Anger

Anger management is a problem for many people in today's world, not only for self-injurers. However, for self-injurers, it is even more so, because self-injury is often an outward expression of suppressed, unacceptable internal feelings. Not being able to control one's anger usually involves, for most people, lashing out at others, for example, verbally or physically. Self-injurers typically lash out at themselves, sometimes exclusively. Sometimes they may also lash out at others, usually either verbally or by giving them the "silent treatment" (suddenly avoiding and not talking to someone, without giving the person any explanation).

First, it is important to acknowledge that one *is* angry. "Okay, so I'm angry—but I don't have to act on it." Many of us, especially girls and women, were taught through our upbringing that anger in itself is a "bad" thing. However, it is just an emotion, just another feeling, and only bad if it is expressed in a negative way (or if it is suppressed and results in ulcers, headaches, etc.).

Then, gain some *understanding* about what made you angry and why. Come up with positive alternative coping strategies for next time. A counselor or therapist can be very helpful with this and may provide you with valuable insights that you may otherwise miss on your own. You may want to ask yourself and write about such questions as the following:

1. What triggering events, memories, associations, thoughts, and other emotions preceded my anger?
2. At what point did I explode? Why?
3. What negative behaviors did I engage in when I was angry (for example, yelled, punched the wall, drank, hurt myself or someone else)?
4. What coping and relaxation skills can I use next time to control my anger (for example, take three long deep breaths, count to ten, take a walk)?
5. Is there a way to *solve* the problem (that I am having at the time)?
6. How can I avoid conflict (with the person I am angry at)?
7. What are the personal consequences of my anger? How has my anger affected me? How has my anger affected my physical health and well-being, including stress? How has my anger affected my mental and emotional health? How has anger endangered me (for example, reckless driving)? How has my anger affected me at work, at school, at home, in the community? How has anger affected me spiritually? (This may include, for example, my relationship with God or my Higher Power, negative behaviors that go against my sense of right and wrong, etc.)
8. What are the consequences of my anger to other people? How has my anger hurt my family, my friends, my spouse or significant other, my co-workers or classmates, people I don't know such as those I pass by in traffic or see in the grocery store?

7. How Self-Injury Has Harmed Me

In Steps Eight and Nine of the Alcoholics Anonymous program, we make a list of all persons we have harmed and to whom we are willing to make amends. The self-injurer may initially think that she did not harm anyone, except for herself, by indulging in this particular type of behavior. However, other people are always affected by our actions, in some way or another, whether it is for good or for bad.

At the very least, self-injury keeps one distant and alienated from other people, even if one does not do anything deliberately or directly to cause harm. Addicts and alcoholics often hear the complaint from family, friends, and significant others, "You weren't there for me!" Perhaps most significant, the self-injurer is harming herself, in a lot of other ways besides just cutting on herself. In recovery, it is therefore very important for her to remember to make amends to *herself* as well as to other people.

In writing about How Self-Injury Has Harmed Me, it is useful to think of the physical, the emotional, and the spiritual. One may ask herself the following questions:

1. How has self-injury harmed me physically (visible scars, burns, damage, bleeding, infections, etc.)?
2. How has self-injury harmed me emotionally (for example, damaged my self-esteem and self-confidence; affected my mental health; increased my feelings of depression and hopelessness and fear; kept me isolated from other people)?
3. How has self-injury harmed me spiritually (for example, addictive behavior becoming more important to me than my relationship with God or my Higher Power and my fellow human beings)?

About a year and a half before my sobriety date, when I was really struggling with making an attempt at recovery and having multiple relapses, I wrote the following list:

How Self-Injury Has Harmed Me

- caused myself physical hurt
- left ugly scars, bruises, and bleeding
- inconvenienced and frustrated by having to hide this by wearing long sleeves, etc., in the hot summer
- inconvenienced and frustrated by having to buy new (actually used, from the thrift store) summer clothes with long sleeves for work, which have been extremely difficult to find and hard on my meager fellowship salary budget
- having the pain of having a secret and feeling separate from and not understood by even my closest friends
- always afraid of "getting busted" by someone who sees my visible battle scars
- always afraid of "getting busted" when trying to find isolated enough places to hide and self-injure
- constant fear of "getting busted" by someone who doesn't understand and getting locked up in a hospital
- last year and a half to two years when it's been real bad, I made sure to keep potential romantic relationships away with recent scars present
- it's gotten in the way of my health—mental: at least I know my self-esteem is low and I *should* stop it but can't—probably physical: I've probably done damage to my nervous system and may have taken years off my life at times when I had to do it to the point of losing consciousness; danger of having a heart attack or stroke at my most escalated; it's left physical damage (burns, scars) all over me
- always the fear recently that it may get worse and one more incident may do me in and I might die and then God wouldn't be too happy with me and I might have to do some time in purgatory or hell

8. My Ideal Day

A useful writing exercise is to think of what your ideal day would be like, including things you like about your life as it is now, and adding or changing things with the goal of striving for how you would ideally like to have it be.

Start with this sentence: "I would wake up at (you name the time) in the morning . . ." and walk through your day, ending with the time that you go to bed at night. For example, Mimi wrote: "I would wake up at 5:30 in the morning because I wouldn't be depressed anymore, have a glass of orange juice, and go for a morning run around the block with my dog." Include whatever you want to, even if it sounds impossible or grandiose (like meeting and marrying a millionaire)—remember, this is "the ideal." Also include simple goals and things you want that are more easily attainable and that you have some control over, and make them happen (for example, "I bought a new CD to listen to on the way home from work"; "I feel better now because I eat healthy most of the time"; "I watched the sunset at 7:30 this evening and thanked God for another day of sobriety"). This makes it more real and likely that good things will happen.

Surprisingly, a lot of people find out, after completing this writing exercise and reviewing what they've written, that they are really a lot happier than they thought they were. Additionally, sometimes the seemingly impossible things do happen, at least on some level. This is because goals, dreams, and aspirations are more clearly stated and you know what you really want and are willing to work for.

9. Things I Like to Do and Things to Look Forward To

Especially when one is feeling down, and ideally on a regular basis, one should make time to do some of the things that she likes to do and can really look forward to. Whether too busy because of work, school, children and household, or whatever your daily routine may be, or not motivated to get up and do much of anything, you should always try to include some fun in your life. This should be something for *you*, by your definition of what is fun and what you enjoy.

Do something in addition to, or at times instead of, those obligations and things people say you "should" do and "should" enjoy doing but do not. Remember, this is about your recovery. For example, twenty-three-year-old Rhonda, a compulsive overeater in recovery, would always feel emotionally drained after visiting her parents every single Sunday for dinner. Her mother and father constantly fought and argued with each other. The truth is, they would have fought and argued with each other whether or not she was there. These Sunday excursions took up most of her day, and working six days a week left her little time for anything else. Being single, Rhonda wanted to spend some time with her friends, have fun, and meet new people. One Sunday afternoon she got an invitation to go shopping with a group of girls from work. Deciding to do something about it was initially difficult, mostly because she felt guilty (or, as she would say, "My parents *made* me feel guilty!"). Eventually, it got easier to think not only about pleasing others, which she naturally did, but also about what was good for her and for her optimal recovery.

You may want to simply make a list of things you enjoy doing (for example, working out, reading mystery novels) and things to look forward to (a vacation on a tropical island, getting in shape physically, etc.). Or, you may want to use the following format, which includes some examples.

I Like/Look Forward To	Last Time I Did This	Action Plan: When, with Whom, etc.
Browsing at a bookstore	About four months ago	Saturday morning for an hour or two before grocery shopping; bookstore at mall; on my own
Go on an African jungle safari	Never	Sometime in the next two years, with my husband when he finishes his project; save money; contact travel agency; get brochures
Gardening	Two or three years ago	Next spring; see what Aunt Nancy did with her garden
Having my nails done	A few weeks ago	Make appointment for this afternoon or tomorrow; see if Alicia wants to go
Watching the sunset	I can't remember	Tonight at 6:30; look out the window

It is important to remember that you do have choices. The exercises in this chapter were designed to give you hope and inspiration for a bright future in your recovery. Keep your journal or notebook handy. You'll be surprised at what it reveals after you review what you've written over time.

CHAPTER TEN

Getting Better

Ten Things That Will Help

There are certain things that every self-injurer needs to do to recover. The same things apply, no matter what treatment option or combination of treatment options are used. Other than points 1 and 2, which need to be first and second, the others may vary in terms of importance for different people and at different times.

In this chapter, the most important points of the book are summarized. Besides points 1 and 2, they are not placed in any particular order of importance. These are as follows:

1. Stop the behavior, and make the *commitment* to stop.
2. Get professional help as soon as possible.
3. Know what to do to slow yourself down in an emergency.
4. Have a strong social support system.
5. Take care of your physical issues.
6. Take care of your emotional issues.
7. Take care of your spiritual issues.
8. Develop a strong sense of self-worth and self-esteem.

9. Acquire knowledge and understanding of this disorder, what you need to do to recover, and what you need to do to maintain your recovery.
10. Have and maintain a positive attitude—get out of the problem and into the solution.

Point 1: Stop the behavior, and make the commitment to stop.

One who is having a serious problem with self-injury may find it very difficult to stop. She may have already tried, a number of different times, in a number of different ways. For example, she may have told herself, her parents, or her boyfriend that she would not do this anymore. Or, she may have tried to reward herself for refraining from the behavior, for example, by purchasing a new short-sleeve shirt that can be worn in the summertime as long as there aren't any new scars on her arms. Sometimes, these things may work temporarily. However, they are not enough in and of themselves to maintain long-term recovery and emotional sobriety.

As with the First Step of Alcoholics Anonymous, "We admitted we were powerless over alcohol—that our lives had become unmanageable," the self-injurer must first admit her powerlessness over the problem of self-injury. This means being totally honest and surrendering. This includes being willing to acknowledge and accept the fact that one is addicted to the feeling, the "high," the vicious cycle of destruction that self-injury brings on.

First, before trying to figure out the exact reasons or trying to tackle the deep-rooted underlying issues in therapy (such as having been abused as a young child), the self-injurer must make the commitment to *stop the behavior.* She must get rid of the symptom, and *stabilize.*

In the same manner that the alcoholic needs to take the

commitment to stop drinking very seriously and with rigorous honesty, the self-injurer must also do so. In the beginning of sobriety, an alcoholic usually disposes of all of the alcohol in the house and may elect to avoid places like bars and dance clubs where the temptation to drink is likely. The drug addict typically disposes of all illicit drugs and drug paraphernalia such as pipes, rolling papers, and hypodermic needles. However, this is much harder for the self-injurer. If she really wants to hurt herself, she can always find a way. Self-injury does not require any money, special materials, or having to go anywhere. There is no need to go to a dark street corner and score from a drug dealer. There is always a place or a way to hide.

The self-injurer needs to make a concerted effort to do the best that she can with this. Making a list of "triggering" material is helpful. Disposing of items that are frequently used to self-injure, such as razor blades, sharp scissors, and knives, are a step in the right direction. Even cutting fingernails down so they can't be used to scratch is a good idea. It is the effort, commitment, and honesty, first with oneself, that counts.

One needs to continue to surrender throughout recovery, to admit being an alcoholic and/or an addict. Every time one walks through the door of a Twelve Step meeting, she is taking the first three Steps. It is customary in Twelve Step meetings to admit that one is an alcoholic or an addict (for example, "Hi, I'm Sharon. I'm an alcoholic and an addict") in front of a group of one's peers. Some self-injurers use the general term "addict" when identifying themselves in meetings that are not specifically for self-injury. This is a viable option.

The self-injurer especially needs to remain verbal and honest and to not think of herself as "better than." This is especially difficult because the self-injurer may, at least initially, view her self-harming behaviors as not quite as "dangerous" or as "bad" as abusing substances like alcohol or illegal drugs. Many self-injurers have concurrent alcohol and/or drug addictions and possibly other behavioral addictions such as anorexia or bulimia. Or, they may have at least *experimented with* or *abused* alcohol and/or drugs. Therefore, it is important to recovery, if not vital, to acknowledge this too.

The first time that I surrendered, I had been driving along a curvy stretch of highway and impulsively burned myself with the cigarette lighter in the car. Yes, I did this while driving. My car swerved into another lane and I almost hit an oncoming car. Along came a police car, complete with flashing lights and siren. I was pulled over. The officer barked at me, "So what do you have to say about your driving? You're all over the road . . . have you been drinking?" I told him no, that I was just extremely upset, my dog just died (I didn't even have a dog), and that I would be more careful. He shone the flashlight in my eyes and made me get out of the car and walk a straight line—which I was able to do perfectly well. He looked at me, completely dumbfounded. The officer suddenly got another call. Reluctantly, he said to me, "I just got an emergency, gotta go. I guess you got off the hook . . . be careful! You could have killed somebody!"

At this point I realized that the effects of self-injurious behavior could be just as harmful as drunk driving. The police officer was right, I could have killed somebody else, or myself, in traffic. As he drove off to his emergency, I finally broke down and admitted to myself and to God, for the first time, that I was an addict. It was, at least, a beginning.

Self-injurers, just like alcoholics and drug addicts, are likely to have repeated "slips" or "relapses," especially in the beginning of sobriety. This is extremely frustrating, for both the addict and concerned others who are trying to help. The addict may be thinking, "Okay, I've tried and I've tried but it's no use; it keeps happening anyway." Each relapse reinforces this negative idea. The extreme self-injurer typically becomes caught in a vicious cycle. This cycle involves having an incident, becoming angry at herself for having done it again, becoming utterly discouraged and hopeless, having a few good days or weeks or months without self injury, then once again becoming overwhelmed by an emotional thought or event, desperately trying to fight off that feeling (the "craving"), and relapsing again.

When a relapse happens, one must

1. Acknowledge the mistake ("Okay, I relapsed") and stop beating up on oneself for being less than perfect.
2. Learn from it.
3. Move on. Get back on track as soon as possible.

Point 2: Get professional help as soon as possible.

The self-injurer must not delay in getting professional help. There are no "quick and easy" solutions to a problem as serious as self-injury, especially when it becomes an addiction.

Trying to do it alone simply does not work. The self-injurer will probably try repeatedly and futilely to go it alone, because she has become so accustomed to isolating herself from other people. She typically isolates herself when having a cutting or burning episode. This hidden behavior is rarely, if ever, done in front of other people. It's not a party thing.

Furthermore, the self-injurer often feels that she is strong, indestructible, and tougher than life—and that she doesn't need anybody. It may therefore initially be very difficult for her to break through this defense, which she may have "perfected" over many years. It is necessary to learn the lesson that part of being independent is knowing when to be dependent.

The self-injurer needs to be open to trying—and combining—different treatment options appropriate to her individual needs. The self-injurer may also have different needs at different times. If medical treatment is necessary (for example, for an infected wound), this must be taken care of first. Martha, a licensed practical nurse who has seen a lot of things in her days, related a story about a woman in her early twenties who had significant problems with self-injury, particularly excessive tattooing. The woman neglected her infection until it was too late—she eventually lost her leg due to gangrene.

There are many different types of treatment choices available for self-injury, as there are for other self-destructive behaviors and addictions. Medical treatment, individual therapy, group therapy, family therapy and/or couples therapy, psychopharmacological medication, inpatient hospitalization, and Twelve Step programs can help. Even within these treatment choices, there are a variety of different techniques and approaches. For example, there are various therapy techniques that may used by an individual therapist, such as cognitive-behavioral approaches, behavior modification, or psychodynamic therapy.

A well-informed, trained therapist who truly understands the emotional dynamics of self-injury can be most helpful. Ideally, the therapist should be a strong, stable person who intuitively knows when to be, and how to combine being, warm and nurturing as well as direct and firm. Such a trained professional will be able to effectively address the addict's denial and defenses.

There are also a number of different types of therapists. For example, many (but not all) adolescent females prefer a female therapist. Maureen, a young college student who came in for alcohol and multi-drug addiction and who also had a severe case of bulimia along with her self-injurious behavior, insisted on a female therapist. She said that she would feel more comfortable talking to another woman about her issues with men and sex.

It is essential that the therapist is knowledgeable about and not afraid of the problem of self-injury. The self-injurer in the beginning stages of recovery is afraid enough herself. She does not need the added stress of having to calm down another person (who is supposed to be helping her) who panics or is taken aback by the sight of blood. Finding the right therapist may take some time, but be patient. It is well worth the effort.

There are no quick fixes out there. Be cautious of medical and psychological "quackery," which is rampant in today's society. Such things may include, for example, noncredentialed "healers," or unproven herbal remedies that claim to "cure" anxiety or depression. Teenagers and young adults may be particularly vulnerable to this.

Point 3: Know what to do to slow yourself down in an emergency.

The progressing urge that precedes a self-injurious episode usually sneaks up on and attacks the person who has the problem of self-injury. This eventually becomes a full-blown emergency that must be stopped before one feels that she is "too far gone" and must self-injure. She's got to slow down.

First, one must recognize the fact that she is in a state of emergency. This is not the time for her, or anyone else, to "analyze" the deep-seated emotional feelings or reasons. If the self-injurer needs to think about or talk about anything, it should only be about facts and events about what happened to set her off. Staying verbal helps.

Different things that are used to slow down and de-escalate work at different times for different people. It helps to make a list of these things, such as using an ice bucket, calling a friend, and finding a "safe place" where an episode will not happen. (See chapter 8 for a more expansive list, along with ideas on what types of things to place on your short list.) It also helps to carry the list around and to refer back to it, at least in the beginning stages of recovery, whenever one gets stuck. This is because, when in an escalated state, the self-injurer becomes emotionally overwhelmed. Especially in the moment of crisis, she just might not be able to see that there are other options, and she may actually forget about the things that work.

At one point when there happened to be a lot of toddlers and young children living in my neighborhood, I would frequently go outside where they were playing. This was a safe place for me. I have never had an episode in front of a child; I always knew that that was an absolute for me. Children are generally happy and don't ask probing questions about your problems and emotions. Being around them always put me in a happier mood, and many times it put me completely back to reset. I would then be able to go back into the house and effectively continue to work on something constructive—my doctoral dissertation.

Furthermore, there is a sense of positive reinforcement in remembering the things that have worked in the past to divert an emergency. For example, one may remember, "Oh, yes, calling my friend Charlene worked last time. I can do that again." Laura, a university hospital nurse with eight years in recovery, whose main problem happened to be heroin addiction among other things, once stated: "Even though I'm going out to dinner with my husband tonight, I do know where an NA meeting is tonight, in case of an emergency and I need one."

Those who are close to or trying to help the self-injurer must respect her needs and realize that she may have different needs at different times. *Ask* her what she needs. Usually, she will tell you. If she does not know, offer but do not force various options.

Point 4: Have a strong social support system.

First, it is important to know that one does not effectively recover or successfully maintain recovery alone. People do need other people, and this is definitely one of those times and one of those situations.

Although the self-injurer may actually prefer to spend most of her time in isolation and to have minimal contact with other people, she needs to get over it. It is helpful for the self-injurer to decide which people are good for her and which ones to avoid.

Just as many alcoholics and drug addicts may need to make new friends because their old drinking and drugging buddies are not good for them, the self-injury addict may need to rethink her social relationships. Frequently, self-injurers have a long history of, and are still at least initially caught up in, a number of unhealthy or destructive interpersonal relationships. Although it may seem hard at first, one needs to make some positive changes. The recovering self-injurer may need to learn how to reach out to others more and how to form new, healthy relationships.

Michelle made an A list, a B list, and a C list and wrote down the reasons why next to each person's name. Having been caught up for many years in unhealthy codependent relationships, she decided to figure out who the people are that she should be around, people whom she needed to avoid because they were bad for her, and people to be cautious around, and least while she was in the beginning stages of recovery. For the first time in her life, Michelle was able to think of taking care of herself first, as the number one priority, because she saw this as vital to her survival.

The A list was defined as "The good people, the ones I should be around." The B list was defined as "People whom I need to proceed with caution around, people I need to get to know better before I trust them, or people whom I can handle only in limited doses." The C list was defined as "Those people I need to avoid no matter what because they're bad for me, and/or those whom I may get tempted to call when I'm lonely, hoping that things were different with them than they actually are." (This included her ex-husband.)

The self-injurer needs to have people whom she can count on, especially in times of crisis. This may include, for example, her therapist, members of her family, close long-term friends, and her priest, rabbi, or minister. If she is in a Twelve Step group, she will have access to other people in recovery, a safe place to go to, and the help of a sponsor if she wants one.

Point 5: Take care of your physical issues.

First and foremost, professional medical treatment must be sought immediately for serious physical problems resulting from self-injury. For example, there may be severely infected scars or burns. A person may need to be rushed to a hospital emergency room, for instance, if she cut her wrists and cannot stop bleeding.

One young model from New York City, who was also a heroin addict, had a serious problem with an infected abscess on her hand. This was initially from a needle injection point. She continually picked at the ever-expanding scab and would not allow it to heal, much like a restless young child who picks at a scab from a skinned knee. The wound finally had to be surgically treated on an outpatient hospital basis.

Many times, what appears to be a suicide may have been an accident. Such a case would be the self-injurer who cuts too deeply or too savagely after having a few drinks and/or an emotional episode.

Self-injurers have typically neglected themselves, which likely includes their physical health, sometimes for many years. Many self-injurers avoid medical doctors altogether because they are afraid that their injuries or scars will be noticed. Furthermore, the self-injurer wants *control,* at least over her own body. Therefore, she may not want anyone to touch her or to tell her what to do, especially when in a vulnerable situation such as in a doctor's examining room. Physical exams and dental checkups should be done regularly and also on an as-needed basis. This is necessary to determine if everything is okay and also to deal with any problems that may be present.

The self-injurer is, of course, at high risk for or may already have problems with alcohol and/or drugs. Drugs may include illegal and/or legal substances, including prescription medication. It is therefore wise to recognize the dangers of and high potential for *addiction substitution.* Self-injurers, just like alcoholics and addicts, are vulnerable to and are sometimes searching for "something" to make them feel better or to escape from their emotional pain.

Physical exercise is important. This will enable a healthy endorphin release and will also promote a feeling of well-being. Many people work out or exercise as a way to vent their feelings of anger and nervous energy. Children regularly go to the schoolyard at recess and at lunchtime; they need to run around and burn off their excess energy so that they can go back to class and refocus on their schoolwork. Prisoners and juvenile delinquents in residential treatment facilities need to exercise to work off their rage and to divert violence.

Physical exercise is a good thing, but one must remember not to overdo it to the point of causing a sports injury. Self-injurers especially need to be aware of this, because their natural tendency is to do just about everything to an extreme.

Healthy nutritional habits are also important. Because self-injurers are at high risk for or may concurrently have eating disorders such as anorexia, bulimia, or compulsive overeating, this is especially important. One should have a healthy diet and, if she is anorexic or overweight, work to attain and maintain a healthy weight.

Good eating habits will also help immensely with self-esteem and self-confidence. Being in good shape physically and making the best of what one has in terms of physical appearance is highly beneficial.

Also, the addict needs to feel that she is taking better care of herself. Making the effort, even if not perfect, is very helpful.

In the beginning days of her recovery, Nancy decided to break her junk-food habit. She went grocery shopping for healthy food and started preparing healthy meals that she could get enthusiastic about. Because she is an excellent cook, an additional benefit was that she could share this with other people in a positive social atmosphere. To this day, with over sixteen years in recovery, Nancy still has a lot of dinner parties at her house.

One may want to consult a qualified medical expert, nutritionist, or a personal trainer at a gym. Reading up on and learning more about health, nutrition, and exercise can also be of great benefit.

A feeling of physical well being, particularly *having consistent physical energy,* is helpful in keeping depressive symptoms to a minimum. This is also effective for helping to decrease the probability of and minimizing the negative effects of the recurring vicious cycle of escalating and de-escalating that is part of the self-injurious behavior syndrome.

Point 6: Take care of your emotional issues.

Self-injury, alcoholism, drug addiction, and anorexia and bulimia are only "symptoms" of the deeper emotional problems and resultant feelings that one is trying to escape. Nicole, a fourteen-year-old anorexic who was also beginning to develop a problem with self-injury, commented: "If only my food and clothes problems would go away, all my problems would be solved." She was at the time still being terrorized and physically beaten by her stepfather on a regular basis.

Sometimes people think that after a thirty-day inpatient recovery stay at a hospital, they are "cured" forever and they don't have to do anything else. Inpatient treatment programs can be a useful way to get jump-started with recovery and a good way to learn the basics of what to do. But by no means is anyone cured after attending such a program. Recovery is a lifelong process, because the vulnerability and the potential to relapse are always there.

People with active self-injury typically have a history of emotional problems. There is a high correlation with child physical abuse, child sexual abuse, neglect, and severe trauma such as rape. However, the self-injury is often hidden—it's a silent addiction.

One profile of a typical self-injurer is someone who is highly intelligent, high achieving, and fully functional (at least for a while, until the self-injury begins to backfire). Most other people see the self-injurer as rather normal, maybe a little bit quiet at times, and they are shocked when they find out she is suffering from this problem. Therefore, the self-injurer may go unnoticed for a long time, maybe forever, unless she somehow gets help.

Lisa, an eleven-year-old girl, was found out when she got upset and lost control one day at school. She repeatedly stabbed and gashed her arm with a pencil, right there in the classroom. She happened to be one of the prettiest girls in her elementary school, was an A student, did volunteer work in the kitchen, and had many wonderful talents such as singing and dancing. Most of the kids in her class, and especially her teacher, were shocked. Only Lisa's two best friends knew about what was going on and about the serious problems with her mother and her grandmother at home.

Emotional issues tend to come up especially during the second year of recovery, after the symptom is gone and the addict becomes stabilized. The recovering addict is typically feeling emotionally raw and ripped open. Self-injurers may be experiencing numerous memories that were previously suppressed. The memories come back, quite vividly, but now with emotions attached to them. At this time especially, a good therapist can be extremely beneficial in providing support and in helping the addict to address and deal with her emotions.

The emotional vulnerability to relapse is, however, always there. Particularly dangerous times are when bad things happen, such as when a family member dies. New experiences that cause anxiety and stress are also difficult, such as when a teenager begins dating. The self-injurer needs to be aware of this and to address emotional issues as they occur, and to learn how to deal with life effectively.

Point 7: Take care of your spiritual issues.

Just as there is a physical and an emotional side to recovery, there is also a spiritual side. It is all very important, if the addict wants to most effectively attain and maintain long-term recovery. Initially, dealing with one's physical issues may be necessary, if not essential, to survival. For example, for an alcoholic, this might include going through detox. Emotional issues tend to come up next, once the addict becomes abstinent and is in the process of learning how to maintain abstinence. All of this takes time and energy.

Spiritual issues usually come up next in the process of recovery. Some people may be able to address and develop their spirituality from the very beginning. They are at an advantage if they are able to do so.

Many addicts, especially while their addiction is active and while in the beginning stages of recovery, are resistant to, or unable to, acknowledge or focus on spiritual issues. Some may neglect spirituality altogether.

Especially these days, people are "searching for something." There is a deep sense of longing within us, be it conscious or unconscious, that cries out for a sense of meaning, of wholeness, and of connectedness with some Power greater than ourselves. Many addicts, including self-injurers, describe chronic feelings of emptiness.

In today's world, problems of poverty, illness, abuse, violence, and all types of other unfairnesses abound. Many attempt to "escape" the resulting feelings by turning to alcohol, drugs, or some other type of self-destructive behavior, trying to fill the void.

It may be especially difficult for those who self-injure to connect with a concept of God or a Higher Power or religion. Refer to chapter 7 for a more detailed discussion of spirituality and recovery from self-injury. Practical suggestions and action steps are offered.

Point 8: Develop a strong sense of self-worth and self-esteem.

When asked the question "How do you feel?" in the beginning stages of therapy, many self-injurers tend to give responses such as, "I feel like I'm a bad person," "ugly," "no good," or "worthless." These things may have been told to them, sometimes repeatedly, by people who have physically, sexually, or emotionally abused or neglected them in childhood or adolescence. The abused or neglected person is likely to internalize these messages. If such issues remain unresolved, it is likely that the victim will repeat this pattern, subconsciously searching for and finding negative relationships with others. This is particularly true regarding romantic relationships.

Self-injurers tend to displace and to take out their anger, rage, and disappointments on themselves, rather than pointing the finger at the negative people in their lives. This may come from, for example, the need to still view a parent who victimized them as a child as ultimately right and ultimately good. An abused child typically feels some sense of dependence on and thus may remain loyal to important figures in her life, such as her mother or father. Many such children, as well as adults, may not know how to, or even be able to, appropriately view and effectively deal with the negativity imposed on them by others.

The self-injurer needs to change her belief system about all this and about herself as a person. She needs to "consider the source" regarding the person or persons who have hurt her in the past. For example, she can ask herself the questions: "Was the person who beat me and told me that I was no good when I was six years old a kind, loving, good, and emotionally stable person for having done so? Was this person being selfish and unfair to have taken out his or her anger and aggression on someone more vulnerable?"

The emotionally wounded person needs to then work on building up her sense of self-esteem and self-worth. This starts with learning how to effectively deal with her own physical, emotional, and spiritual issues.

It is important to remember that humility is honest appraisal; it is not self-denigration. Everyone has both good qualities and things that they can improve on.

Brandon, a client who was assigned to me for therapy at a hospital outpatient clinic, had numerous addictions and was in the early stages of recovery. He had exceptionally low self-esteem and a profound lack of self-confidence at the time, although he was handsome, successful, and a recent graduate from a culinary arts program at a prestigious school. He landed a spectacular, high-paying job as a chef at one of the city's finest restaurants. However, he was apprehensive about the fact that this was his first job, and that he was much younger and less experienced than the others at his workplace. Brandon also happened to be working on his Fourth Step as part of his AA program, which involves writing a moral inventory. Because of his tendency to think only of the negative and to beat up on himself, I suggested that he also make a list of his good qualities, and of the things that he has done well in his life. This was much harder for him. However, he did so successfully and also fared well at his new job.

In Twelve Step programs, people in recovery are frequently told to "stick with the winners." You are encouraged to find and associate with other people who, ideally, have what you would like to have. One can look at people who are positive, happy, self-assured, and who have high self-esteem, and can learn something from them. My first sponsor, with twenty-four years in recovery at the time, had and continues to have those qualities, which I could aspire to.

It would be of great benefit for recovering self-injurers, or any addict, to target and focus on their good qualities. It also helps to pursue an activity that you like and are good at. Such activities may include, for example, sports, music, or art. This will build self-esteem and self-confidence that will carry over to other areas of your life.

Point 9: Acquire knowledge and understanding of this disorder, what you need to do to recover, and what you need to do to maintain your recovery.

You are already off to a good start by reading this book. There are a few books that are available at bookstores and libraries on the topic of self-injury. There are also numerous clinically sound journal articles on this topic in the fields of psychology, psychiatry, medicine, and social work that can be found at university libraries.

One can learn a lot from reading literature on alcoholism and substance abuse, which is prevalent and readily available. This includes books, journal articles, and Twelve Step literature on substance abuse. Because self-injury is an addictive disorder, many of the dynamics involved and methods of recovery that can be used are the same as for addictions to alcohol or drugs.

The self-injurer may also want to learn more about those things in her background that may have led to the problem of self-injury, and about other related factors. This may include, for example, the literature on child abuse, trauma, anorexia, codependent relationships, depression, or post-traumatic stress disorder.

The Internet can also be a valuable resource for learning more about self-injury and also about other addictions. But one must beware that there is also some negative and potentially very harmful information on self-injury out there as well. Such information is usually found on the Internet and in various "underground" newsletters and publications. This type of literature and these particular Web sites are written by and tend to draw people who are voyeuristic or who glorify and do not want to give up the thrill or the high associated with the self-injurious behavior syndrome. Additionally, some material may contain disturbing "triggering" material that is detrimental, with a focus on gory, sensational, and horrifying images. Some material even "glamorizes" the disorder.

A well-trained and knowledgeable therapist or medical expert can help the self-injurer to better understand herself and what is going on. A therapist can also help the self-injuring client to set and work toward achieving appropriate goals for herself and for her recovery.

A lot can be learned from other people who have recovered successfully and are maintaining their recovery. This may include others who are in recovery for self-injury, as well as those in recovery from alcoholism, drug addictions, or eating disorders. Twelve Step groups such as Alcoholics Anonymous, Narcotics Anonymous, and Overeaters Anonymous are good places to find such people. Because of the exceptionally high correlation between self-injury and eating disorders, people who currently have or who have had problems with self-injury are frequently found in Overeaters Anonymous meetings, especially in the ones that focus on anorexia and bulimia.

Point 10: Have and maintain a positive attitude— get out of the problem and into the solution.

Most self-injurers, as well as many alcoholics and addicts, come from backgrounds of extreme childhood physical and/or sexual abuse, emotional abuse, neglect, or violent households with alcoholic or addicted parents. Or, they may

have endured trauma such as rape. The addict may therefore be inclined to see herself in the role of the "victim."
This can generalize to any situation in her life, including seeing herself as the victim of this unfair and misunderstood affliction of self-destruction.

There is a lot to be said about the power of positive thinking. One must get out of the cycle of negativity and hopelessness. The vast amount of literature on mind-body medicine
speaks of how a person's state of mind, belief system, and
will to survive can positively or negatively affect the outcome
of virtually any disease. This is true for all of the addictive
disorders as well, including self-injury.

I have been working clinically for many years now with
children and teenagers who are juvenile delinquents and on
probation, as well as with those who have been removed
from their homes and are under the care of the county
because they were abused, neglected, or come from unsafe
home environments. All of them have come from horrendous backgrounds.

Oftentimes, I have told these kids that I'm very sorry that
they had to go through what they had to go through—for example, something as traumatic as having been abused as a
child—and that it was unfair and not their fault. Since it's
not possible to turn back the hands of time, they need to acknowledge and learn from the past and then move on. It is
now time for them to do what they can do. They are here
now, with the rest of their lives ahead of them. They now
have the power to make decisions about, and to set goals
for, the kind of life that they want to have—and to do something about it.

Christina, a sixteen-year-old pregnant girl, was placed by
the court system in a residential treatment facility for pregnant and parenting teens. Her mother had died, and her father had abused and then abandoned her when she was a

young child. She took to the streets, because she had no place else to go.

Christina got involved with drugs and other negative things and with a gang-affiliated boy who got her pregnant. The boy did not want anything more to do with her or the baby, and he was nowhere to be found. The one person whom Christina thought she could count on, her stepmother who lived in another state, promised that she would be there with her at the time of delivery. The stepmother failed to show up and later told her that she couldn't make it because she got busy with her new job at the post office.

To further complicate matters, Christina went through a very traumatic and painful ordeal in childbirth. The baby's umbilical cord was wrapped around his neck, and he almost died. Fortunately, Christina was able to focus on and be grateful for the fact that her beautiful new son had survived and that he turned out to be healthy. She decided that she wanted better for her child than what she had had for herself.

Right after the birth of her son, Christina became very depressed for a while, so much so that it was difficult for her to get out of bed in the morning and go to school. Because she was far behind in her academic credits due to her life on the streets, Christina for some time had the attitude that it was of no use to even try, that she would never be able to graduate from high school anyway. She was beyond discouraged.

With the tireless help of the clinical staff and her therapist over a period of time, Christina began to develop an increasingly more positive attitude and outlook. She decided that she wanted better for herself too. She made up her mind and moved forward. Her therapist helped her to set goals. Christina graduated from high school, turned eighteen, and enrolled in college—with a scholarship in hand—to pursue a career as a registered nurse.

"Get out of the problem and into the solution" is a popular

saying in AA and other Twelve Step groups. It is a good attitude to have toward life in general. Other people have done
so successfully. Twelve Step meetings that are positive,
upbeat, and solution-focused can be especially valuable to
anyone. They are particularly valuable to those addicts and
self-injurers who have had, or who currently have, problems
with getting out of their negativity.

Afterword/Response from Readers

We are interested in hearing from those who would like to share their knowledge, experience, strength, and hope to help self-injurers and other addicts who are still out there struggling. We are particularly interested in hearing from those who are getting results from this book.

If you are a self-injurer (whether recovered or thinking about it), a parent, educator, medical or mental health professional, or a concerned other, please write to us. If you know of someone interested, please ask him or her to review a copy of this book and write to us also.

Responses will be kept confidential/anonymous. Consolidated material from readers' responses may be used in a forthcoming book by the author/researcher to further our knowledge and understanding of self-injury. It is not possible to respond individually to the overwhelming number of personal appeals that we anticipate may result from this book. Let us reiterate that *Secret Scars: Uncovering and Understanding the Addiction of Self-Injury* is to be used as a resource; it is not a substitute for the self-injurer seeking treatment and professional help as necessary.

Respond to:

V. J. Turner
c/o Hazelden
P.O. Box 176
Center City, MN 55012-0176
v.j.turner@hazelden.org

References

Alcoholics Anonymous World Services, Inc. 1976. *Alcoholics Anonymous.* 3d ed. New York: Alcoholics Anonymous World Services, Inc.

American Psychiatric Association. 1994. *Diagnostic and statistical manual of mental disorders.* 4th ed. Washington, D.C.: American Psychiatric Association.

Bell, R. 1985. *Holy anorexia.* London: University of Chicago Press.

Benson, H. 1975. *The relaxation response.* New York: Avon Books.

Bergmann, G. H. 1846. Ein Fall von religioser Monomanie. *Algemeine Z Psychiatrie* 3:365–80.

Briere, J. 1996. *Therapy for adults molested as children.* 2d ed. New York: Springer.

Briere, J., and E. Gil. 1998. Self-mutilation in clinical and general population samples: Prevalence, correlates, and functions. *American Journal of Orthopsychiatry* 68 (4): 609–20.

Callender, A. 1999. *Pathways through pain.* Cleveland, Ohio: Pilgrim Press.

Chein, I. 1964. *The road to h: Narcotics, delinquency, and social policy.* New York: Basic Books.

Clark, R. A. 1981. Self-mutilation accompanying religious delusions: A case report and review. *Journal of Clinical Psychiatry* 42 (6): 243–45.

Connors, R. 1996. Self-injury in trauma survivors: Functions and meanings. *American Journal of Orthopsychiatry* 66 (2): 197–206.

Conterio, K., and W. Lader, with J. K. Bloom. 1998. *Bodily harm: The breakthrough healing program for self-injurers.* New York: Hyperion.

Cross, L. 1993. Body and self in feminine development: Implications for eating disorders and delicate self-mutilation. *Bulletin of the Menninger Clinic* 57 (1): 51–68.

Doing time, doing Vipassana. 1997. Karuna Films, Ltd. Videotape.

Dulit, R., M. Fyer, A. Leon, B. Brodsky, and A. Frances. 1994. Clinical correlates of self-mutilation in borderline personality disorder. *American Journal of Psychiatry* 151 (9): 1305–11.

Egan, J. 1999. Power suffering. *New York Times Magazine* 16 May: 108.

Favaro, A., and P. Santonastaso. 2000. Self-Injurious behavior in anorexia nervosa. *The Journal of Nervous and Mental Disease* 188 (8): 537–42.

Favazza, A. 1987. *Bodies under siege: Self-mutilation in culture and psychiatry.* Baltimore: Johns Hopkins University Press.

———. 1989. Why patients mutilate themselves. *Hospital Community Psychiatry* 40:137–45.

———. 1992. Repetitive self-mutilation. *Psychiatric Annals* 22 (2): 60–63.

———. 1998. The coming of age of self-mutilation. *The Journal of Nervous and Mental Disease* 186, no. 5 (May): 259–68.

Favazza, A., and K. Conterio. 1988. The chronic plight of self-mutilators. *Community Mental Health Journal* 24, no. 1 (Spring): 22–30.

———. 1989. Female habitual self-mutilators. *Acta Psychiatr Scand* 79:283–89.

Favazza, A., L. DeRosear, and K. Conterio. 1989. Self-mutilation and eating disorders. *Suicide and Life-Threatening Behavior* 19 (4): 352–61.

Fenning, S., G. Carlson, and S. Fenning. 1995. Contagious self-mutilation. *Journal of the American Academy of Child and Adolescent Psychiatry* 34, no. 4 (April): 402–3.

Friedman, H. L. 1989. The health of adolescents: Beliefs and behaviour. *Social Science and Medicine* 29 (3): 309–15.

Fulwiler, C., C. Forbes, S. L. Santangelo, and M. Folstein. 1997. Self-mutilation and suicide attempt: Distinguishing features in prisoners. *Journal of the American Academy of Psychiatry and the Law* 25 (1): 69–77.

G. and C. Merriam Co. 1979. *Webster's new collegiate dictionary.* Springfield, Mass.: Merriam-Webster.

Gardner, A. R., and A. J. Gardner. 1975. Self-mutilation, obsessionality and narcissism. *British Journal of Psychiatry* 127:127–32.

Green, A. H. 1978. Self-destructive behavior in battered children. *American Journal of Psychiatry* 135 (5): 579–82.

Grof, C. 1993. *The thirst for wholeness: Attachment, addiction, and the spiritual path.* New York: HarperCollins.

Hazelden. 1975. *Twenty-four hours a day.* 2d ed. Center City, Minn.: Hazelden.

Herman, J. L., J. C. Perry, and B. van der Kolk. 1989. Childhood trauma in borderline personality disorder. *American Journal of Psychiatry* 146 (4): 490–95.

Jones, A. 1986. Self-mutilation in prisons: A comparison of mutilators and nonmutilators. *Criminal Justice and Behavior* 13, no. 3 (September): 286–96.

Kelly, J., and M. Kelly. 1996. *Sanctuaries: The complete United States.* New York: Bell Tower.

Khantzian, E. J. 1985. The self-medication hypothesis of addictive disorders: Focus on heroin and cocaine dependence. *American Journal of Psychiatry* 142:1259–64.

———. 1990. Self-regulation and self-medication factors in alcoholism and the addictions: Similarities and differences. In *Recent Developments in Alcoholism,* edited by M. Galanter (New York: Plenum Press, 255–71).

Kriesman, J. J., and H. Straus. 1991. *I hate you, don't leave me: Understanding the borderline personality.* New York: Morrow, William, and Co.

Lacey, J. H., and C. D. Evans. 1986. The impulsivist. *British Journal of Addictions* 81:641–49.

Linehan, M. M. 1993. *Cognitive-behavioral treatment of borderline personality disorder.* New York: Guilford Press.

Lipschitz, D. S., R. K. Winegar, A. L. Nicolaou, E. Hartnick, M. Wolfson, and S. Southwick. 1999. Perceived abuse and neglect as risk factors for suicidal behavior in adolescent inpatients. *The Journal of Nervous and Mental Disease,* 187:32–39.

Menninger, K. 1934. A psychoanalytic study of the significance of self-mutilations. *Psychoanalytic Quarterly* 4:408–66.

———. 1938. *Man against himself.* New York: Harcourt Brace.

Morgan, H. 1979. *Death Wishes?: The understanding and management of deliberate self-harm.* New York: John Wiley and Sons.

Pao, P. 1969. The syndrome of delicate self-cutting. *British Journal of Medical Psychology* 42 (3): 195–206.

Pattison, E., and J. Kahan. 1983. The deliberate self-harm syndrome. *American Journal of Psychiatry* 140, no. 7 (July): 867–72.

Regalbuto, R. J. 1998. *A guide to monastic guest houses.* Harrisburg, Pa.: Morehouse Publishing.

Rosen, P. M., and B. W. Walsh. 1989. Patterns of contagion in self-mutilation epidemics. *American Journal of Psychiatry* 146 (5): 656–58.

Schneider, J., and B. Schneider. 1991. *Sex, lies, and forgiveness: Couples speak on healing from sex addiction.* Center City, Minn.: Hazelden.

Shilling, L. E. 1984. *Perspectives on counseling theories.* Englewood Cliffs, N.J.: Prentice-Hall.

Simeon, D., B. Stanley, A. Frances, J. Mann, R. Winchel, and M. Stanley. 1992. Self-mutilation in personality disorders: Psychological and biological correlates. *American Journal of Psychiatry* 149 (2): 221–26.

Simpson, C. A., and G. L. Porter. 1981. Self-mutilation in children and adolescents. *Bulletin of the Menninger Clinic* 45, no. 5 (September): 428–38.

Sinetar, M. 1986. *Ordinary people as monks and mystics: Lifestyles for self-discovery.* Mahwah, N.J.: Paulist Press.

van der Kolk, B., J. C. Perry, and J. L. Herman. 1991. Childhood origins of self-destructive behavior. *American Journal of Psychiatry* 148, no. 12 (December): 1665–71.

Walsh, B. W., and P. Rosen. 1988. *Self-mutilation: Theory, research, and treatment.* New York: Guilford Press.

Weber, T. 1998. Despair of the "system kids." *Los Angeles Times,* 21 May.

Yalom, I. D., 1985. *The theory and practice of group psychotherapy.* New York: Basic Books.

Young, E. B. 1990. The role of incest issues in relapse. *Journal of Psychoactive Drugs* 22 (2): 249–58.

Zaidens, S. 1951. Self-inflicted dermatoses and their psychodynamics. *The Journal of Nervous and Mental Disease* 113:395–404.

Zlotnick, C., M. Shea, P. Recupero, K. Bidadi, T. Pearlstein, and P. Brown. 1997. Trauma, dissociation, impulsivity, and self-mutilation among substance abuse patients. *American Journal of Orthopsychiatry* 67, no. 4 (October): 650–54.

Index